A Trekkers Guide To :

THE HILL TRIBES
OF NORTHERN
THAILAND

By John R. Davies
assisted by Tommy Wu

GW00758974

Footloose books,
5, Bridge Street,
SALISBURY
Wiltshire
England

Footloose books.
© John R. Davies 1990
1st edition 1989
2nd Edition 1990

ISBN 0-9516496-0-4

Published by Footloose Books, 5, Bridge Street, Salisbury, Wiltshire . England.
Printed in Thailand by Chang Puak Press, 149 Chang Puak Road, Chiang Mai 50000 Tel. (053) 221810
Distributed by Roger Lascelles, Cartographic and Travel publishers, 47, York Road, Brentford, Middlesex TW8 0QP England.

John Davies has lectured in Social Biology and Anthropology at colleges in Britain and the United States. He has travelled widely in South East Asia, and has developed a deep respect for the hill tribe peoples.

Tommy Wu was born in China and migrated with his family into Burma. His father was a Lisu headman.He speaks four of the hilltribe languages fluently and is amongst the most knowledgeable and respected of hilltribe guides.

For my son Jonathon

I would like to thank the following people for their help in the making of this book: My guides and translaters Tommy Wu, Vacharin Sirichai and My Lee. The staff of the Hill Tribe Research Institute, Chiang Mai University. Nick Greenwood and Graham Osborn for their assistance with the text. My particular thanks go to all the headmen and peoples of the hill tribes who gave freely of their time to answer all my questions with good humour and patience.

CONTENTS

INTRODUCTION

Like all societies, the hill tribes of Northern Thailand are going through a period of sudden and tremendous change. Their cultures, which they have stubbornly protected against outside influences for thousands of years, are currently facing the challenge of existing in a world of shrinking resources and expanding populations, of deforestation, loss of soil fertility and exploitation. The integration of the hill tribes into Thai society is now advancing rapidly. It is doubtful if, under all these pressures, it is possible for the integrity of hill tribe societies to be maintained for more than a few years.

This book describes the traditional way of life of the hill tribes. In some areas these traditions are still strictly adhered to, in others some of these have already faded. Many villages practise their traditions supplemented by modern alternatives - it is common, for example, for a hill tribe patient to take two aspirin after a ritual curing ceremony. In Christian villages Christ may be regarded by the villagers as another spirit to add to their list.

Anyone who has spent time with the hill tribe people will be aware that their way of life has much to teach us. It cannot be denied that modern health care, education and organization have benefited the hill tribes enormously, but the inevitable dilution and ultimate dissolution of these ancient cultures is a high price to pay.

PRACTICAL INFORMATION

WAYS TO SEE THE HILL TRIBES
One day visits

Much the most comfortable and convenient method. There are serious disadvantages, but if you are short of time, or not keen or capable of some physical exertion, does give a flavour of the hill tribes and the chance to photograph hill tribe people in their traditional costumes and setting. The villages you will see must, of course, be very accessible to the big towns and near a road. The villagers will see many tourists every day, and will obtain much of their income from tourism. You need not worry about taking photographs, but do expect to pay for the privilege. Villagers will probably actively try to sell you handicrafts and are unlikely to treat you to the traditional hospitality you would receive in a more remote village.

Excursions

These tours take two or three days. You will probably not have to walk for more than two or three hours each day. Excursions are included in many package tours, and the itinerary is fairly fixed, so do not expect to see any remote, untouched villages. Tourists are a common sight in these villages, and a significant source of their income. A rafting or boat ride and an elephant safari are usually included.

A common tour from Chiang Mai would be: Four hour bus ride; 3 hour boat trip on the Mae Kok river to a Karen village where the group will spend the night. The next morning a two hour elephant ride to a Mien village, 1 hour walk to a waterfall, Two hour walk to an Akha village where you will stay overnight. The next day a two hour hike to a Shan village, then return to Chiang Mai by bus or jeep.

Trekking tour

These generally take from four to six days. They may visit quite remote areas, so you may see villages that have not been exposed to westerners for very long. These trips can be much the most authentic way of experiencing the life of the hill tribes but be prepared for some discomfort and effort. You will probably be sleeping on bare floors and the jungle is your toilet. Trekking may take up five hours or more of most days, and may involve quite steep ascents and descents. Boots that support the ankle are advisable, since there is considerable strain put on them. It is not necessary to be exceptionally fit, but if you are very out of condition or have any physical problems you might consider another option. How good the experience turns out to be depends largely on the guide and organization. There are many tour agencies in Chiang Mai, and some in Chiang Rai and Mae Hong Son. The best way to ensure a good guide is to talk to them before signing up and to ask people who have been trekking recently how it went. The best guides originate from the hill tribes, speak one or more of the hill tribe languages and have a good command of English. Remember that you may be many miles from western facilities such as medicines, and that you are heavily reliant on your guide for several days, so its important to be in good hands. Find out from him beforehand exactly where you are going, how you will get there, how long each day you have to hike (perhaps adding one hour on to what he says !) what the terrain and weather will be like, how many are in the tour group, meals, what you will be expected to carry and anything else you consider important.

Most tour agencies supply you with a small backpack for essentials. These should include one change of clothing, sun hat, salt tablets, insect repellant, antiseptic, anti diarrhoea medicine, plasters, sun lotion, toilet paper, torch, soap, tooth brush and tooth paste. It is advisable to take a bed sheet if possible, and a sleeping bag or extra blanket in the winter months. Deposit valuables in your hotel or guest house safe, after making a written note, signed by the staff, of exactly what you are leaving behind. For added security, hire a safe deposit box from one of the major banks. It is a good idea to take a photocopy of your passport with you. The cost of a typical four day tour varies between 1,000 and 2,000 baht (1990'). This includes all expenses except drinks in the villages. Many tour operators limit the amount of money you take with you (perhaps 200 baht). This prevents too much cash entering the villages and undermining their economy, and makes the tours less of a target for bandits. Every trek is registered with and monitored by the tourist police.

Hiring a private guide

This is probably the best way of getting to know the hill tribes and gaining some insight into their lives. It is more expensive - at least 500 baht per day, but worth it to many. On the debit side, you miss out on the camaraderie and sociability that usually develops between the members of a group tour.

Individual trekking

Many tourists, either on foot or motor bike, plan their own itinerary and wander the hills, staying where they can.

This makes for the most adventurous and exciting trip, but does have real dangers and cannot be recommended. Several people have been killed in the hilltribe areas recently. Which areas are safe and which not is subject to constant change. A few tourists have wandered into Burma and had great difficulty getting back to Thailand. The chances of being robbed are quite high. You should only attempt these trips if you are experienced and have done some research into the geography and economics of the areas you hope to visit. Ask for advice at the Hill Tribe Research Institute, Chiang Mai University.

Without a guide, you run the risk of offending the hill tribes by your behaviour. It is very easy to unwittingly cause offence. In most villages it will be impossible to communicate except by sign language, so be aware and sensitive to the effect you seem to be having, and read the etiquette section of this chapter very carefully.

You will usually be provided with the veranda of the headmans hut to sleep on, or the schoolhouse if there is one. You should offer payment for the accommodation (30 - 50 Baht) and any food you eat (5 - 10 Baht).

The chances of getting lost are high. There are no accurate maps of the region and little signposting. If you are getting around on a motor bike bear in mind that the paths to most villages are narrow, steep and stony, so only experienced motor cyclists should attempt them. In the wet season most paths are unfit for any traffic. It will be very difficult to

3

get treatment for any injury sustained through coming off the bike. Riders have been shot or had their bikes stolen in the hills.

If you do decide to travel independently, use the maps in this book to find you way to the most accessible hilltribe villages.

WHEN TO GO

There are three seasons in the north of Thailand - cool and dry (October to February), hot and dry (March and April), warm and wet (April to September)

1. Cool and dry. The best time for trekking. Temperatures during the day are 24 - 28 degrees C (depending on altitude). At night it can be very cool, sometimes close to freezing. The vegetation is lush after the wet season, but there is virtually no rain during these months.

2. Hot and dry. Temperatures during the day are in the high 30s, at night 8 - 12 degrees C. The vegetation is dried up, many trees have lost their leaves, and the countryside is very dry and dusty. Forest fires are frequent and you may have to walk in a quite unpleasant smoky, hot, dusty atmosphere. The rivers are low so rafting is not as much fun as at other times of the year.

3. Warm and wet. During the wet season it may rain on most days, but usually only in the evenings and at night. Nevertheless, paths are always wet and muddy and the high humidity makes walking uncomfortable. River levels make rafting exciting if not dangerous ! Daytime temperatures reach about 30 degrees C, at night it is usually above 20 degrees C.

HEALTH

You should have protection against hepatitis, malaria, polio, typhoid and cholera. Never drink unboiled water unless it has been treated with sterilizing tablets and avoid fresh fruit and vegetables. Use antiseptics on any cuts, and take plasters. Use insect repellant lavishly. Do not bathe in fresh water, especially still water, as many unpleasant parasites can be caught this way.

HILL TRIBE ETIQUETTE

The culture of the hilltribes is often incomprehensible to the western mind. To integrate fully with the villagers is impossible, but having said that, all peoples have attributes in common and communication, although difficult, is very rewarding. The smile is a friendly expression throughout the world, as are many other facial movements. Act in a soft spoken and respectful way, and remember that in a hill tribe village you are the student and the villager is the teacher. Learning to say 'hello', 'goodbye', 'please' and 'thank you' will be much appreciated. Use the phrases section of this book to learn these and other expressions and words in each hilltribe language. Do not be too inquisitive, respect the privacy of the villagers and only take photographs after asking permission. Open displays of affection between girlfriend and boyfriend are offensive, as is the western habit of removing most clothes when the sun shines ! Within hilltribe houses, the altar is particularly sacred and should never be touched or abused. Do not attempt to sleep under or near it. A star shaped bamboo sign outside a house (usually above the main door) means that permission should be asked before entering.

KAREN

Foreigners are normally only received on the veranda. The stumps of the burnt trees in the swiddens are taboo to touch.

HMONG (MEO)

You should not enter a Hmong house unless invited to do so by a male inhabitant. This does not apply if no Hmong men are in the house.

MIEN (YAO)

The stoves within Mien houses should not be touched or leaned against as spirits reside in them.

LAHU (MUSOR)

The sacred posts around the temple are a source of blessing, and should not be touched.

AKHA

You must never touch the gates at the entrances to Akha villages. You must accept any offer to enter a house, and must take the drink or food offered to you. A common delicacy is mouse. The greatest honour is to be offered dog soup. Men should never enter the womens section of an Akha house.

LISU

Guests may not enter the bedrooms, touch the altar or sleep with their heads towards the fire. Men and women cannot sleep together as the altar is in the guest room. No-one should stand in the doorway with their feet either side of it.

GEOGRAPHY OF TREKKING AREAS

The hills and mountains of Northern Thailand are the furthest south eastern extension of the Himalayas. This range of mountains, the most massive in the world, is of recent geographical origin, so has not suffered the softening effects of erosion for too long. This results in dramatic sharp peaks and valleys rising suddenly from the flat plain that surrounds these hills. The contrast between the endless flat rice paddies of the lowlands and the steep wooded uplands they surround is a characteristic of the landscape of Northern Thailand. A number of rivers carry the high rainfall of the mountains to the Maekhong, the 9th longest river in the world, and the largest in South East Asia. This river forms most of the border between Northern Thailand and Laos in the east. In the far west of Northern Thailand rivers empty into the Salween river which forms the western border with Burma (Myanma). This river flows through Burma and empties into the Bay of Bengal. The Maekhong reaches the South China Sea in Vietnam. The Mae Kok river forms a natural barrier across Northern Thailand. The area north of this river is generally called the 'Golden Triangle' although for touristic reasons this term is often applied to the point at which the borders of Burma(Myanma), Thailand and Laos meet on the Maekhong river. North of the Mae Kok deforestation and over farming have produced a ravaged upland landscape of almost bare hills with small patches of forest overlooking the fertile plains.

The Ping river, on which Chiang Mai is situated, runs south, emptying into the Chao Praya near Bangkok. It separates Northern Thailand into a western section of high mountains and deep valleys, sparsely populated and relatively unspoilt and inaccessible. East of the river the land is flat and fertile with a dense scattering of farming villages and a few larger towns. There is one central range of hills before a range of higher mountains which mark the Laos border.

The natural vegetation of the entire area is tropical dry forest. The long dry season from October to May prevents lusher rain forest from developing. At low elevations the density of trees is lower and trees are smaller, except close to streams and rivers. As one ascends, trees increase in size and density as rainfall increases. Some patches of

7

cloud forest are found at the greatest altitudes, eg the peak of Doi Inthanon. Here the trees are covered in epiphytic ferns and mosses and temperatures below freezing are not uncommon in the winter.

The predominant underlying rock type is limestone. Water erosion has caused the formation of a number of caves and waterfalls, some very beautiful, which are scattered throughout the hills.

Hill tribe villages are almost always found at altitudes above 500 metres, although there are a very few at lower elevations. Since they are also the most accessible, they tend to be heavily touristed. In general, these lower villages have become partly integrated into Thai society and are losing their cultural identity to some extent. Many people of hill tribe origin, particularly Karen, are living as Thais in lowland towns and villages.

CHIANG MAI

Chiang Mai is the second largest city in Thailand, with a population of over 1.2 million. It has excellent road, rail and air links with the rest of the country and is going through an unprecedented boom at the moment, as tourists and Thais alike try to escape the pollution, traffic congestion and overcrowding of Bangkok. Known as the 'Rose of the North' Chiang Mai is noted for its relaxed pace of life and friendly people. Despite its rapid growth, it is still a very pleasant city to stay in, and the main centre for hill tribe trekking. There are currently over 200 agencies selling treks, although, particularly in the low season, they will team together to achieve a viable number of tourists to make the treks profitable.

The city is built on the banks of the Ping river, which rises in the hills to the north and flows into the Chao Praya river at Nakhon Sawang. To the west of the river the mountains rise suddenly from the narrow alluvial plain, and apart from a few narrow valleys continue to the Burma (Myanmar) border. The mountain of Doi Pui, altitude 1685 metres, is only 15 kilometres from Chiang Mai. To the north narrow valleys are intersected with ranges of hills reaching south. To the east valleys are wide and fertile, with occasional ranges of mostly low hills. South of Chiang Mai sparsely inhabited hills and valleys reach to the Salween river in Burma (Myanma). To the south east the valleys widen out as the hills give way to the hot fertile plains of central Thailand.

Within 20 kilometres of Chiang Mai there are very few hill tribe villages. One exception to this is Doi Pui, a Blue Hmong village five kilometres beyond the beautiful temple of Doi Sutep which overlooks the city. Although the setting of this village is very lovely , its proximity to Chiang Mai has made it a popular destination for a half day trip from the city, with consequently a huge number of visitors. In the last few years the village has deteriorated to little more than a large open air supermarket for hill tribe products. The Hmong villagers have become caricatures of themselves, begging from the tourists and charging for photography poses.

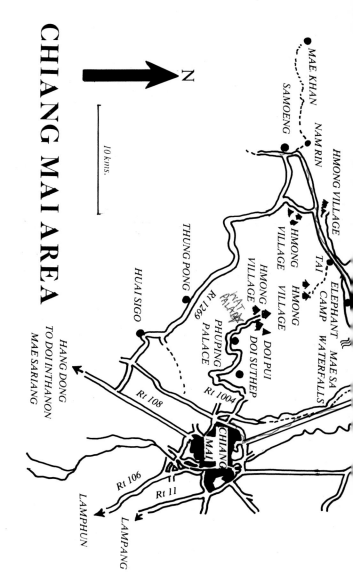

CHIANG MAI AREA

N

10 kms.

MAE KHAN

SAMOENG

NAM RIN

HMONG VILLAGE

TAI

ELEPHANT

CAMP

MAE SA

WATERFALLS

HMONG
VILLAGE

HMONG
VILLAGE

HMONG
VILLAGE

WAT
PALARD

PHUPING
PALACE

DOI PUI

DOI SUTHEP

Rt 1269

THUNG PONG

HUAI SIGO

HANG DONG
TO DOI INTHANON
MAE SARIANG

Rt 108

Rt 1004

CHIANG
MAI

Rt 106

Rt 11

LAMPHUN

LAMPANG

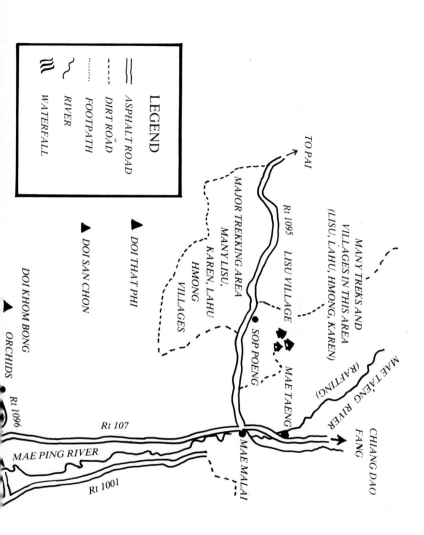

LEGEND

ASPHALT ROAD

DIRT ROAD

FOOTPATH

RIVER

WATERFALL

▲ DOI THAT PHI

▲ DOI SAN CHON

▲ DOI KHOM BONG

ORCHIDS

TO PAI

Rt 1095   LISU VILLAGE

MANY TREKS AND
VILLAGES IN THIS AREA
(LISU, LAHU, HMONG, KAREN)

MAJOR TREKKING AREA
MANY LISU,
KAREN, LAHU
HMONG
VILLAGES

SOP POENG

MAE TAENG

MAE TAENG RIVER
(RAFTING)

CHIANG DAO
FANG

Rt 107

MAE MALAI

Rt 1096

MAE PING RIVER

Rt 1001

11

Lakes and mountains near Chiang Dao. This view is typical of the scenery of the north of Thailand, where rugged jungle clad mountain ranges alternate with flat fertile valleys.

MAE SA

The Mai Sa valley is only 20 kilometres north of Chiang Mai, but is an area of outstanding natural beauty and interest, remarkably unspoilt despite its proximity to a major city. It contains many 'tourist traps' - there are several elephant camps, butterfly farms and orchid nurseries on the itinerary of every tour operator in Chiang Mai, and a number of 'resorts', wooden or bamboo bungalows set in tropical gardens, ranging from cheap and basic to expensive and luxurious. Several Hmong and Karen villages are located in the hills above the valley, and although rather exploited and non traditional are an interesting destination for an elephant ride.

The valley is reached by travelling north along Route 107 15 kilometres to just beyond Mae Rim, then turning west along Route 1096. After 5 kilometres there is a left turn to the beautiful Mai Sa waterfalls. Most of the tourist attractions are in the next 15 kilometres, between the villages of Mae Mae and Tai. After Tai the road rises steeply out of the valley and continues west through glorious mountain scenery with views to the uninhabited mountain ranges stretching to the horizon. Close to the road there are three Hmong villages worth a visit. 20 kilometres from Mae Rim is the pretty little mountain town of Samoeng. Route 1269 leads south east from here through undisturbed mountain jungle to join route 108. Turn north here to reach Chiang Mai, or south to Doi Inthanon.

CHIANG DAO

This small town is 70 kilometres north of Chiang Mai on route 107. The town itself is unexceptional, but is dominated by Chiang Dao mountain which looms over the town. Although at 2175 metres its altitude is less than that of Doi Inthanon, it is a more impressive sight because of its sudden emergence from the plains. Beneath the mountain there are a number of caves. The largest is Chiang Dao cave, reached by a small road leading west from route 107. This series of caves contain Buddhist temples and images and are of great religious importance to Thais.

With their beautiful location and mystical aura they should not be missed.

North of Chiang Dao the scenery is some of the most dramatic in Thailand. Saw toothed pillars of rock covered in dense foliage rise abruptly from the plains and mountain streams flow into reed fringed lakes. There are a number of Lisu, Lahu and Hmong villages in this area, but the activities of opium sumgglers make it dangerous to travel here without a guide.

To the south of Chiang Dao mountain is a favourite area for trekking. The hill tribes here are unspoilt and friendly, and the Mae Tang river is convenient for rafting. Lisu, Hmong, Karen and Lahu villages are found in this area.

THE GOLDEN TRIANGLE

This area, with its long association with opium and heroin production, is bounded by the Mae Kok river to the south and the Mekhong river to the East, which is also the Laos border. To the north is the Shan state of Burma (Myanmar).

The Mae Kok river rises in the mountains of Burma (Myanmar) and flows into the Mekhong just south of the town of Chiang Saen. About half way along the river is the large city of Chiang Rai, the usual gateway to the Golden Triangle. Although growing very rapidly with an increasing number of tourists, the city itself has little to interest the visitor. It does, though, make a good base for exploring the Golden Triangle area.

Trips along the Mae Kok by ferry, long tail boat and bamboo raft are popular. There are a number of hill tribe villages along the river upstream. There is a boat which sails daily to Thaton, a small and pleasant town close to the Burmese border - boats can also be hired here to travel downstream.

The town of Mai Sai marks the border with Burma, and the northernmost point of Thailand. The bridge over the small stream separating Thailand from Burma is one of the few land links between the two countries. Thais and Burmese cross this border freely, but westerners are forbidden

Long tailed boats on the Maekok river at Thaton. Trips west to Chiang Rai can be taken by bamboo raft or boat. In the rainy season this gentle stream becomes deep and fast flowing.

15

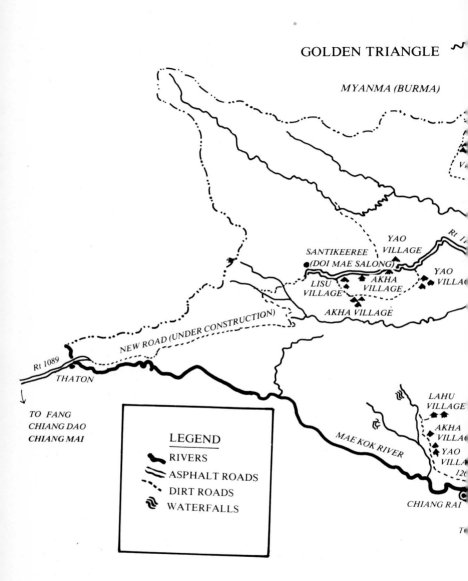

GOLDEN TRIANGLE

MYANMA (BURMA)

YAO VILLAGE

Rt 1...

SANTIKEEREE
(DOI MAE SALONG)

AKHA VILLAGE

YAO VILLA...

LISU VILLAGE

AKHA VILLAGE

NEW ROAD (UNDER CONSTRUCTION)

Rt 1089

THATON

TO FANG
CHIANG DAO
CHIANG MAI

LAHU VILLAGE

AKHA VILLA...

MAE KOK RIVER

YAO VILLA...

120...

CHIANG RAI

T...

LEGEND

RIVERS

ASPHALT ROADS

DIRT ROADS

WATERFALLS

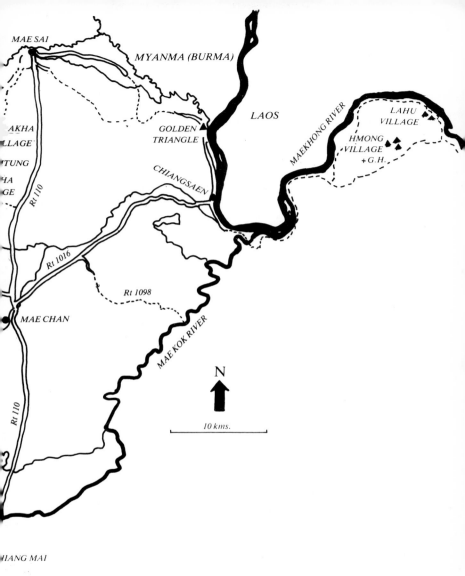

MAE SAI

MYANMA (BURMA)

LAOS

AKHA
VILLAGE
TUNG
HA
GE

Rt 110

GOLDEN
TRIANGLE

MAEKHONG RIVER

LAHU
VILLAGE

HMONG
VILLAGE
+ G.H.

CHIANGSAEN

Rt 1016

Rt 1098

MAE CHAN

MAE KOK RIVER

Rt 110

N

10 kms.

CHIANG MAI

from entering Burma here, and tourists foolish enough to wade across the shallow stream frequently end up in a Burmese jail ! The town is a major shopping area for imported Burmese goods, and for the sale of fake 'Burmese' goods (especially gems) to naive western tourists. The town has a strange frontier feel to it, and a pretty temple on a hill giving fine views into Burma.

The road from Chiang Rai to Mai Sai (Route 110) separates the Golden Triangle into two distinct regions.

West of the road the hills contain a dense hill tribe population. Most of the Akha villages in Thailand are in this area, but Lisu, Yao, Karen and Lahu villages can also be found. The high population density has led to massive deforestation, so most of the hills are bare of trees, giving a desolate appearance of brown earth and dead tree stumps in the dry season. In a very few years further slash and burn farming will be impossible as nutrients will have gone and topsoil will have washed away into the streams and rivers.

The main road from Mae Chan to Doi Mae Salong passes several Akha and Yao villages, but their accessibility and convenience for the tour buses from Chiang Rai has turned these villages into little more than collections of souvenir stalls. In these villages traditional costumes are worn, but you will be asked for money to take photographs.

The majority of the population of the town of Doi Mae Salong are Chinese refugees from the communist revolution of 1949. They are called 'Kuomintang' and are the remnants of the army which fought against the communists. The town has a distinctly Chinese flavour, and is picturesquely perched on a high ridge looking out over the hills of Burma (Myanmar).

The most visited area is just north of the Mae Kok and a few kilometres west of Chiang Rai. All the villages in this area see a great number of tourists, many of whom stay overnight, and it is not unusual to find the tourist population in a village exceeding the hill tribe population. However, tourists are well catered for, with elephant rides and river rafting available.

East of the Chiang Rai - Mae Sai road the countryside is pleasant, with a dense scattering of mainly Thai villages. A small range of low hills

The Maekhong river between Chiang Khong and Chiang Saen. The ninth longest river in the world and the longest in Southeast Asia, it flows from Tibet along the Burma, Laos and Thailand borders across Kampuchea and Vietnam to the South China Sea.

separates these lowlands from the Maekhong river. The 'Golden triangle' itself is on the river 8 kms north of Chiang Saen. The spot is marked by a cement painted arch, through which can be seen a narrow strip of Burma to the west of the Maekhong, separated from Thailand by the small Mae Sai river. Across the wide Maekhong to the east is Laos. The road is lined with souvenir stalls and guest houses for about 500 metres either side of the 'Golden Triangle' arch. Long tail boats will take you on a high speed tour of the 'Golden Triangle' passing close to the banks of the three countries.

Chiang Saen, south of the 'Golden Triangle', is a pleasant town from which boat trips can be taken along the Maekhong. To the East the river narrows as it flows between hills on either side, and becomes more scenic, with rock formations rising out of the river in the dry season. A good laterite road closely follows the course of the river between Chiang Saen and Chiang Khong, a pretty town noted for its annual catch of 200 + kilogramme catfish in May.

The hills in this area are less deforested than further west, and contain a number of little visited Yao and White Hmong villages. The Hmong in this area have migrated recently from Laos, and some are involved in plots to overthrow the government of Laos and establish a Hmong homeland there.

DOI INTHANON

The Doi Inthanon National Park is seventy kilometres south west of Chiang Mai. It has an area of 48,000 hectares and includes the highest point in Thailand at 2565 metres. The lowland areas are farmed, and hill tribe slash and burn agriculture has removed much of the primary forest below 2,000 metres. Above this height the dense forest is festooned with vines and tree living ferns. Several species of rhododendrons are common here. The road through the park is excellent.

The main river running through the park is very good for swimming, particularly behind the information centre, and has along its length some beautiful waterfalls, including the highest in Thailand with a 250 metre plunge. Mae Klang waterfall is a favourite spot for visitors, with a large pool suitable for swimming and a number of food and

Mae Klang waterfall, Doi Inthanon. These waterfalls are a popular tourist spot, with cafes and a large natural swimming pool just below the falls.

drink stalls. There are many hill tribe villages in the area, mostly Karen but some Hmong. Although close to Chiang Mai and accessible by good laterite roads, these villages are little exploited for their tourist potential and are traditional and hospitable. Within the National park there are a number of beautifully situated bungalows and houses for rent at low cost. These can be booked at the park headquarters.

A few kilometres from the summit of Doi Inthanon is a sharp turn off west to the small pretty town of Mae Chaam. The road winds down a steep and precipitous ridge with stunning views of mountains and steep sided valleys. From Mae Chaam a recently improved road leads south to the Hot - Mae Sariang road. Travelling west along this road, a number of very interesting and little visited Pwo and Sgaw Karen villages can be found.

MAE HONG SON

Arguably the prettiest town in Thailand, Mae Hong Son is situated 180 kilometres north west of Chiang Mai. The town has a lovely situation, surrounded by high mountains and built around a quiet and pretty lake, and makes an excellent base for touring the unspoilt and very beautiful countryside. There are several good hotels and guest houses to stay in, and some excellent restaurants. Until recently Mae Hong Son was a sleepy, undeveloped town, but in the last two years tourism has grown enormously. This has led to an improvement in facilities but not yet to the over commercialisation that has affected many parts of Thailand.

The town is overlooked by a steep hill with a lovely Burmese style temple (Doi Kong Mu) at the summit. There are two interesting Burmese influenced temples around the lake.

The population of Mae Hong Son is only 2% ethnic Thai. Almost half are of hill tribe origin, the rest being Shan or 'Thai Yai' (mixed Shan and Thai).

Hill tribe villages in this area are traditional and little visited, providing the most revealing picture of hill tribe life. There are many Karen

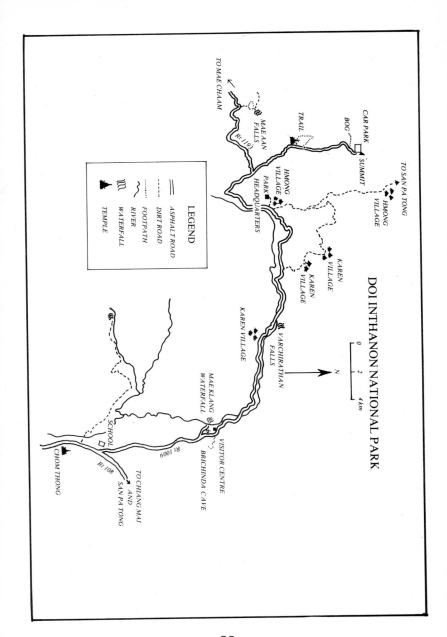

DOI INTHANON NATIONAL PARK

LEGEND

ASPHALT ROAD
DIRT ROAD
FOOTPATH
RIVER
WATERFALL
TEMPLE

TO MAE CHAAM

MAE AAN FALLS
R1 1193

TRAIL

BOG

CAR PARK

SUMMIT

TO SAN PA TONG

HMONG VILLAGE

HMONG VILLAGE

PARK HEADQUARTERS

KAREN VILLAGE

KAREN VILLAGE

KAREN VILLAGE

VARCHIRATHAN FALLS

MAE KLANG WATERFALL

SCHOOL

VISITOR CENTRE

BRICHINDA CAVE

R1 1009

R1 108

CHOM THONG

TO CHIANG MAI AND SAN PA TONG

0   2   4 km

N

Lisu, Lahu and Hmong villages, but no Akha or Yao. Near Mae Hong Son is a Padong Karen village. These people are noted for the womens fashion of lengthening the neck in childhood through the use of gold hoops. These 'long-neck' women are a major tourist attraction, but there are currently only three who still have the long necks. They charge a large amount for photographs !

Until recently the area was inaccessible. In 1965 a tarmac road was completed linking the town with Mae Sariang, then through Hot to Chiang Mai. This indirect route is still the only completed road link from Chiang Mai, involving a 9 hour bus drive. There is a more direct route through Pai, but the road from Pai is not surfaced so is very slow and uncomfortable. Thai Airways have a frequent and inexpensive plane service to Mae Hong Son which is an attractive alternative.

PHAYAO

This pleasant town is overlooked by most tourists, but has much of interest and makes a good base for exploring some remote and isolated hill tribe villages. Within a few kilometres there are Lisu and many Yao (Mien) villages, and a little further afield villages of the other hill tribes can be found.

Phayao is built on the remains of a bronze age settlement, but has twice been abandoned, finally being resettled in 1840 by emigrants from Lampang. It was a walled city, but the remains of these walls are not now visible.

The town is built on the shores of a large natural lake, with a high mountain, Doi Bussaracum, opposite. There are a number of excellent restaurants on the shores of the lake, which could be turned into a water sports resort centre in the future.

NAN

Situated in the extreme east of the area, Nan is an important trade centre with nearby Laos. The city itself is not of great interest to the tourist, but the hills close to the Laos border contain a fascinating and little explored mixture of hill tribes. Nan province is the only area where the H'tin, Kha-mu and Mlabri (Phi Tong Luang) people can be found.

ORIGINS AND DISTRIBUTION

All the hill tribes have migrated into Thailand in comparatively recent times - forced across the borders by civil war, political pressures or simply a need to expand into new areas. This migration is still continuing, albeit at a low level, from Laos and Burma.

KAREN

The Karens have lived in Burma for many centuries. According to legend, they were founded over 2600 years ago, possibly between Tibet and the Gobi desert. 200 years ago they began to migrate into Thailand, and successive waves have crossed the border periodically ever since. They are the largest of the hill tribes, with a population of about 300,000 in Thailand and 4. 8 million in Burma. Their villages are distributed along the Thai border as far south as Bangkok, with their heaviest concentrations west of Chiang Mai. North and East of Chiang Rai there are few villages.

HMONG

The Meos (Hmong) originate from South China, possibly from the mountains of central Asia before this. Their present population is about 70,000 in over 250 villages, mainly close to the Laotian border, North and West of Chiang Mai and South of Tak.

MIEN

The Mien (Yao) originated in Southern China over 200 years ago. According to their legends they migrated 'across the waters' to Hainan, where peoples closely resembling the Mien still live. There are about 40,000 Mien in Thailand, 1.3 million in China and 200,000 in Vietnam. The migrations into Thailand began about 150 years ago, predominantly from Laos, which has only a small population remaining. Most of their villages are close to the Laotian border, around Chiang Rai and around Nan.   25

Origins and distribution

LAHU

The Lahu (Mussur)   migrated into Thailand from North east Burma from
about 1880 on. They originated in South west China, in Yunnan, and some
speak Yunnanese. There are about 55,000 Lahu in Thailand, 150,000
in Burma and 250,000 in China. Almost all their settlements are concentrated
along the Burmese border, north of Chiang Mai ·

AKHA

The Akha people originated south of Kunming in Yunnan province,
South China. They have been migrating south for centuries, the first
village appearing in Thailand in 1903. Their population is about 28,000,
their villages are found in a fairly small area north of Chiang Rai.

LISU

The Lisu believe they were the only humans to survive a great flood.
They originated in Eastern Tibet, and the first settlers arrived in Thailand
in 1921. Their population in Thailand is now 24,000. There are Lisu
villages in China, Burma and North east India, but none in Laos or
Vietnam. Their villages are close to the Burmese border north of
Chiang Mai and West of Chiang Rai.

KAREN SETTLEMENT AREAS

BURMA

Kok river

LAOS

Khong river

ping river

FANG

CHIANG
RAI

CHIANG
DAO

PHAYAO

Salwear river

MAE HONG
SONG

CHIANG
MAI

NAN

LAMPHUN

Ping river

LAMPANG

PHRAE

Sirikit
reservoir

UTTARADIT

LOEI

Phumiphol
reservoir

Yom river

Nan river

Pa Sak river

Moi river

TAK

SUKHO
THAI

PHITSANO
LUK

PHETCHA
BUN

KAMPHAENG
PHET

PHICHIT

NAKHON
SAWANG

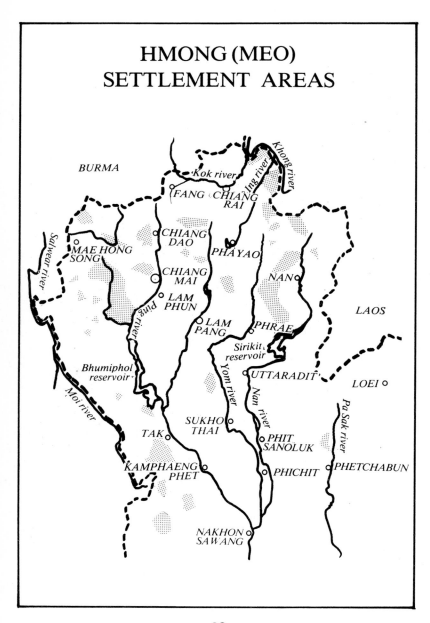

HMONG (MEO)
SETTLEMENT AREAS

BURMA

Kok river

FANG

CHIANG RAI

Ing river

Khong river

CHIANG DAO

MAE HONG SONG

Salwear river

PHAYAO

CHIANG MAI

NAN

LAM PHUN

LAOS

LAM PANG

PHRAE

Ping river

Sirikit reservoir

Bhumiphol reservoir

UTTARADIT

LOEI

Yom river

Moi river

Nan river

Pa Sak river

SUKHO THAI

TAK

PHIT SANOLUK

KAMPHAENG PHET

PHICHIT

PHETCHABUN

NAKHON SAWANG

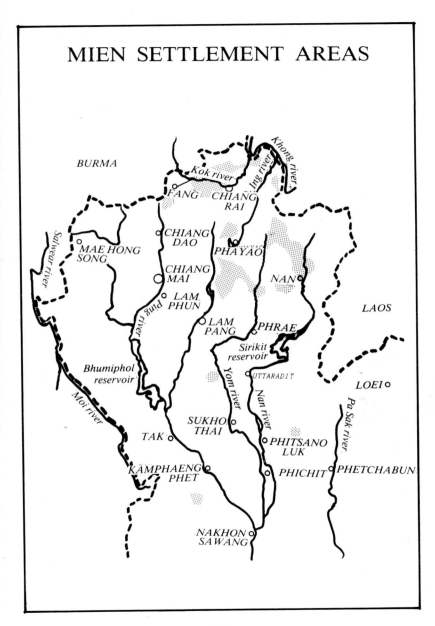

MIEN SETTLEMENT AREAS

BURMA

Kok river

FANG

CHIANG RAI

Ing river

Khong river

CHIANG DAO

PHAYAO

Salwear river

MAE HONG SONG

CHIANG MAI

NAN

LAOS

LAM PHUN

Ping river

LAM PANG

PHRAE

Sirikit reservoir

Bhumiphol reservoir

UTTARADIT

LOEI

Moi river

Yom river

Nan river

Pa Sak river

SUKHO THAI

TAK

PHITSANO LUK

KAMPHAENG PHET

PHICHIT

PHETCHABUN

NAKHON SAWANG

AKHA SETTLEMENT AREAS

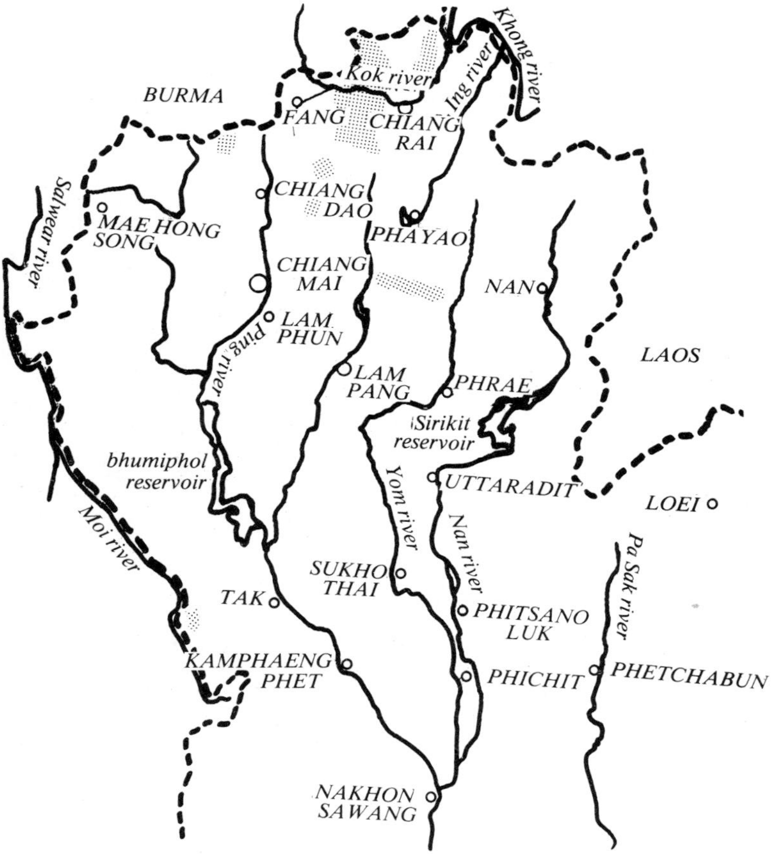

BURMA

Kok river

Ing river

Khong river

FANG

CHIANG RAI

CHIANG DAO

Salwear river

MAE HONG SONG

PHAYAO

CHIANG MAI

NAN

Ping river

LAM PHUN

LAOS

LAM PANG

PHRAE

Sirikit reservoir

bhumiphol reservoir

UTTARADIT

LOEI

Moi river

Yom river

Nan river

Pa Sak river

SUKHO THAI

TAK

PHITSANO LUK

KAMPHAENG PHET

PHICHIT

PHETCHABUN

NAKHON SAWANG

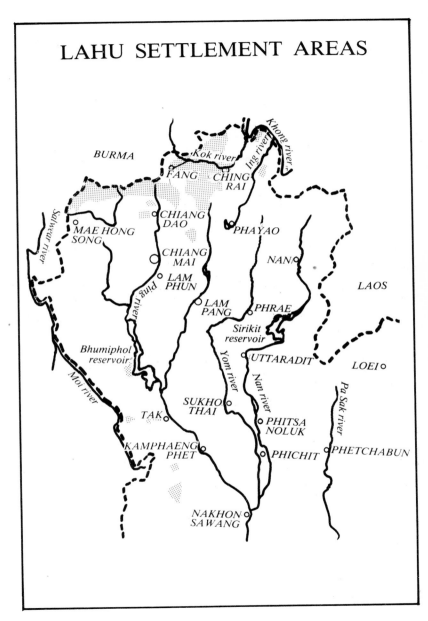

LAHU SETTLEMENT AREAS

BURMA

Salwen river

Kok river

Ing river

Khong river

FANG

CHING RAI

CHIANG DAO

MAE HONG SONG

PHAYAO

Ping river

CHIANG MAI

NAN

LAM PHUN

LAOS

LAM PANG

PHRAE

Sirikit reservoir

Bhumiphol reservoir

UTTARADIT

LOEI

Moi river

Yom river

Nan river

Pa Sak river

TAK

SUKHO THAI

PHITSA NOLUK

KAMPHAENG PHET

PHICHIT

PHETCHABUN

NAKHON SAWANG

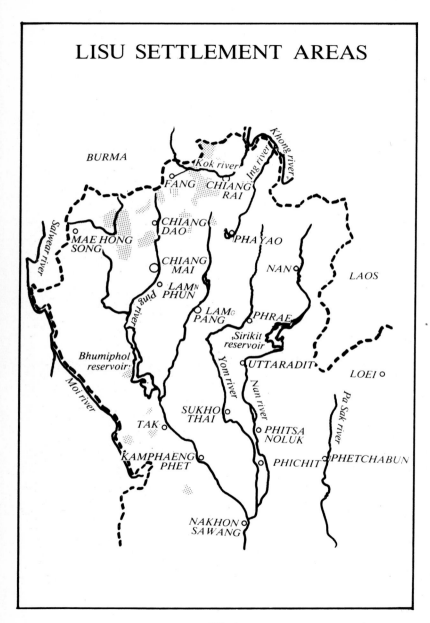

LISU SETTLEMENT AREAS

BURMA

Kok river

FANG CHIANG RAI

Ing river

Khong river

CHIANG DAO

PHAYAO

Salwear river

MAE HONG SONG

CHIANG MAI

NAN

LAOS

LAMᴺ PHUN

Ping river

LAMᴳ PANG

PHRAE

Sirikit reservoir

Bhumiphol reservoir

UTTARADIT

LOEI

Moi river

Yom river

Nan river

Pa Sak river

SUKHO THAI

TAK

PHITSA NOLUK

KAMPHAENG PHET

PHICHIT

PHETCHABUN

NAKHON SAWANG

Pwo Karen unmarried girls wear an enormous number of bangles and beads throughout the day. This headmans daughter spends much of her evenings weaving her elaborate clothes.

COSTUME AND HANDICRAFTS

The most obvious and remarkable characteristics of the hill tribes are their colourful, exquisitely crafted costumes and the beauty of their adornments. Their skills can also be seen in their tools, utensils, weapons, basketry and musical instruments.

Each tribe has a unique range of styles and colours particular to it. Great pride, time and imagination is exercised in the production of clothes and jewellery. They are an expression of status, pride and art. Until recently, traditional costumes where worn at all times, with the most ornate costumes kept for ceremonial occasions. Nowadays western clothing - shorts, jeans and T shirts are worn by many men and children for everyday use, particularly in the more accessible villages, but traditional clothing still predominates amongst the women.

Many everyday articles are produced by each household; others are made by specialists working within the village. Women make clothes, whilst men make tools and weapons. Specialist blacksmiths and silversmiths have high status in the village, and skilled ones may attract people from considerable distances.

Jewellery will commonly be made of silver, although brass, copper and aluminium will also be used. Silver is the common currency amongst the hill tribes, as they do not trust paper money. Animals, land, wives and crops will all be paid for with silver. Spare silver functions as a bank account, often displayed around the body of a hill tribe woman fashioned into ornaments.

Clothing and crafts are not generally regarded as marketable products. They may, however, attract sales from other villages or tribes, and recently their potential as items for tourists has been recognized. There are now three organizations sponsoring the production of hill tribe crafts, realising their possible contribution to the hill tribe economy.

KAREN

Karen women are outstanding weavers. Their use of colour produces very beautiful garments. The use of seeds in their embroidery and emphasis of seams creates unusual effects.

Skaw Karen elder: enjoying a pipe of tobacco and looking after his grandchildren whilst his children work in the fields.

Karen costume

The upper garments of men, women and children are made in the same way. They consist of two strips of hand woven cloth. The strips are folded in half, the fold forming the shoulders. They are then stitched together, leaving openings for head and arms which are bound with braid of contrasting colours. Weaving is done on simple back strap looms using a single warp technique.

The two subgroups of the Karens - Sgaw and Pwo - wear different styles of clothing. Unmarried girls wear a long white cotton shift. Since they make their own clothes, they are simple in young girls and become complex and ornate as the girls become more proficient and adventurous. Sgaw girls weave a band of pink or red just above the waist, but Pwo girls add on red diamond shaped patterns from knee or waist to hem. Sometimes a red yoke will be added. The hair is worn long, tied in a knot on the top of the head. Young women and adults tie their hair in a bun, with two possible sorts of head covering - a red or white turban with a long fringe or a veil tied round the head hanging loose over the shoulders. Married women wear sarongs and over blouses in a wide variety of designs. Blouses may be of indigo dyed cotton or woven with predominently red colours in diamond patterns. Jobs tears seeds may be woven into the pattern and may form a major part of the overall effect. Strips or rectangles of gold, blue or green colour may add to the contrast of the garment.

Married women wear sarongs made of two strips of material sewn together horizontally and stitched together to make a tubular skirt, held up with a cord or metal belt. They vary from knee to ankle length. They may be completely tie-dyed or contain strips of tie-dyed material, sometimes of rich colours with red usually predominating.

Mens shirts hang to the hips. They are usually made of red homespun cotton with yellow or blue stripes. The braiding around the neck is of red, green and blue thread.

Sarongs or Thai peasant style trousers are worn. The knee length sarongs are made of two panels, white or red with one blue stripe in each panel. Trousers reach to mid calf.

Men wear turbans of silk or cotton, red or undyed. Young Pwo men before marriage wear their hair long and pulled tightly in to knot over one ear.

Hmong elder wearing the traditional band of silver.

Hmong women sew and embroider in every spare minute. The sewing machine has greatly increased their output.

The skill and imagination of Hmong embroidery is famed throughout Thailand.

HMONG

Hmong women are famous for their exquisite embroidery. Everyone from baby to the aged will have some rich embroidery somewhere on their costumes. Cloth is generally purchased from traders, but many women prefer to spin their own cloth from hemp or cotton.

The most delicate work is reserved for the clothing of their babies. The carrying cloth is made of two rectangular pieces of material of unequal size joined at the borders, the smaller on top. Red straps tie the baby onto the back. The top triangle is ornamented with cross stitch embroidery, applique and tiny pink pompoms. Caps vary greatly from clan to clan, but all are elaborately ornamented in great detail.

Blue Hmong women wear pleated short skirts reaching to the knee. Batik methods are used to produce the patterns, which are drawn onto the cloth in beeswax. The cloth is then immersed in cold indigo dye which stains all but the beeswax areas. The wax is then removed by boiling and the skirt can be dyed again. An apron is worn over the skirt, black for everyday use but highly decorated ones are worn at all ceremonial occasions. Sometimes several red sashes will be worn over this plus a silver belt. Jackets are of black velvet or cotton. Decoration can be either an embroidered or appliqued strip down the lapels or a zigzag strip diagonally down from the right shoulder. Collars are rectangular, stitched to the jacket with the embroidered side down. Leggings of black or white cloth are worn from knee to ankle. The hair is swept forward and tied in a bun, covered in a black and white checked cloth. The skirts of white Hmong women are of white hemp cloth with no adornment. The collars on the jackets are highly embroidered and appliqued at the back. Black aprons edged with blue are worn front and back. Ceremonial ones are adorned with decorative central panels and tassels. The head is shaved above the ears and thick turbans of various kinds are wound around the hair which is tied in a bun above the forehead. Hmong men wear baggy black pants secured usually with a leather belt. Jackets may be made of cotton, velvet or silk. They are ofter collarless and fasten at the front with silver buttons. They may be very short, reaching just below the chest. Long embroidered sashes are worn around the waist, leaving the ends hanging over the front like an apron. The head is shaved and most wear a black satin skullcap.

Much Hmong wealth is kept in the form of silver jewellery. All the family silver is worn at the new year festival. Earrings in the design of arrows, S shapes or hooks are common. Heavy engraved silver bracelets are worn, as well as neck rings and pendants of butterflies, bells, fish, wheels or balls. Hmong women wear many silver rings.

MIEN (YAO)

A very popular display of wealth is to have the teeth capped with gold. Mien women wear loose fitting trousers, ankle length tunics, sashes and a turban. Black or indigo are the predominating colours. Ideally clothes are made of home grown cotton, but more commonly the cloth will be bought from the Thai. The main part of the trousers is heavily embroidered by the women in five standard designs in shades of red, blue, gold and sometimes green. Apart from the five standard patterns, the embroidery is up to the imagination of the individual. Many threads and dyes may be used.

The tunic is split at the waist and made of three pieces. There is a prominent ruff of bright red wool and an embroidered border extending almost to the waist. There may be silk and bead tassels extending from the split sides. The turban is wide and sometimes wrapped around a red top cloth. The embroidered ends frequently stick up from the turban. Men wear a loose fitting jacket that crosses over the chest and is fastened with silver buttons. Loose fitting indigo trousers reach to below the knee. Younger mens jackets are decorated with red, blue and white edging and decorative patches forming pockets. Babies and small children wear richly embroidered caps with pink or red pompoms.

On special occasions women and children wear silver neck rings, with silver chains extending down the back to which are attached silver ornaments. The tunic may also be decorated with silver jewellery and coins for ceremonial use.

The Yao are also noted for their embroidery, especially the imaginative designs used on their trousers and turbans

Lahu men frequently work as labourers for other hill tribes. This Lahu man has been cutting wood for a nearby Lisu village.

This Lahu women from a village near Mae Hong Son is clearly suspicious of the camera.

Chicken sacrifices are a cure-all in Lahu culture. This woman is preparing a chicken to cure her ailing son.

LAHU

The different subgroups amongst the Lahu wear very different costumes. The Lahu Nyi women wear short lined jackets, long skirts and leggings of blue cotton. Jackets are edged with red down the front, bottom and upper arms. Bands of blue and white are also used. They are closed with large buckles. Skirts are worn folded in front held up with a metal belt or sash. They have three horizontal panels. Red top and bottom with blue, black or black and red stripes in the centre. Men wear loose black jackets fastened at the sides and loose black or indigo trousers reaching to the calf.

Lahu Sheh clothing is made of heavy black cotton. Women wear calf length tunics with yellow or white edging and embroidered coloured sleeves. They are closed with silver buckles to the waist. The black trousers are trimmed with red and yellow stitching and reach to the knees. Men and women wear black turbans, but recently flowered designs and white turbans are becoming popular. Men dress in loose fitting black jackets with elbow length sleeves.

The Lahu Na ankle length tunic is trimmed with predominantly red embroidered designs. The sleeves have narrow bands of red and other colours. There is a diagonal piece from the throat to under the right arm, encrusted with silver buttons. Under the tunic is a black sarong with strips of brightly coloured cloth in various patterns. A black turban is decorated with beads and tassels. Lahu Na men wear black cloth suits. Jackets open in front or down the sides, and the trousers are ankle length and loose fitting. Jackets and trousers are decorated with lines of red thread.

Atchoo wears her magnificent Akha head-dress with pride. It is in two parts, the bottom half is never removed.

The Akha blacksmith is highly respected, and takes pride in his skill. Typically one blacksmith will service several villages.

AKHA

The Akha womans costume consists of a very ornate head dress, a jacket worn over a halter like garment, a short skirt, a sash with decorated ends and leggings. The hip length jacket is made of two strips of cloth with seams down the back and sides. Sleeves are long and straight. The front is plain, the back has a lower panel of intricate design in gold, red and blue. The knee length skirt hangs low on the hips, straight at the front and heavily pleated at the back. The halter is variable in design, often short enough to leave the midriff bare. A sash is tied around the waist and weighted with buttons, coins and beads. Leggings are made of embroidered indigo cloth. Headdresses are magnificent in their design and execution. There are three basic types. The U Lo-Akha head dress has two main parts. The base is a wide head band decorated with silver beads, buttons and coins. On top of this is a cone of bamboo covered with indigo cloth, coated with silver ornaments, beads, feather tassels, furs and anything that the owner deems suitable.

The Loimi-Akha headress is flatter and has alternate layers of beads and silver buttons over the crown. Strings of silver balls and chains hang down to the shoulders. The Phami-Akha headress is completely encrusted with silver coins, buttons and balls. It is helmet shaped with red strings of beads hanging down to the shoulders from back and sides.

Mens jackets are loose and black. They attach at the front with a single button. The central front panel is intricately patterned with red and gold blocks and stripes of colour. The lower back panel is similarly embroidered. A wide turban is worn on the head, often with a black and white design.

These Lisu girls show the typical good humour of their tribe. Their gaudy costumes are now usually made of synthetic fabrics, but retain the traditional colours and patterns.

LISU

The clothing of Lisu women is very brightly coloured. At ceremonial events, the richer women wear impressive amounts of heavy silver ornaments and jewellery. The use of synthetic materials is now common. A blue or green tunic, split up the sides to the waist, is knee length in

The costumes worn by young Lisu women at their New Year festival are arguably the most beautiful and spectacular in the world. The solid silver vests are a chance to show the wealth of the family. Dancing will continue for three days without a break in this nuptual extravaganza.

front, calf length at the back. The chest piece is a different colour from the rest. Bands of bright colour are strung from the black yoke. The lower sleeves are always red but narrow strips of bright colour are sewn above this. Beneath the tunic knee length trousers are worn. Below these leggings of many colours are worn. A wide black sash is tied around the waist, with many coloured threads with pompoms at the bottom suspended from it in two groups. Hair is tied at the back, but turbans are used for ceremonial occasions. They are black and tightly rolled into a hoop of cloth. Many strands of brightly coloured yarn are attached to the turban and hang down to the shoulders. At new year festival young women wear great amounts of silver jewellery strung from a special waistcoat and a cloth collar with silver buttons and dangles attached. Wide silver bracelets are worn on both wrists and silver rings on the fingers.

Men wear a black jacket which opens diagonally or vertically. Coloured threads may be strung from the base for ceremonies, and the tunics may be embellished with rings or silver buttons. Blue or green trousers and black leggings may be worn. A red sash is tied around the waist. Traditional turbans are now rare, replaced by a white towel folded over a piece of cardboard. A silver earring is worn in the left ear, and silver bracelets on each wrist.

The Pwo Karen headman is both a religious and administrative leader. A chicken sacrifice made by him has particular significance.

51

MYTHS, LEGENDS AND RELIGION

These are discussed together as they are inextricably linked, and crucial to every aspect of hill tribe life. Few activities of any importance can be considered before the relevant spirits have been consulted, assuaged or propitiated. Hill tribe people are constantly vigilant against any actions that could offend their gods. As visitors, it is helpful to be aware of the most important taboos, although any minor infringements are considered indulgently, as tourist behaviour seems to be beyond the consideration of the local supernatural agencies !

The hill tribes are all predominantly Animists-that is they believe that conscious spirits with powers over humans exist in many of their surroundings. There are spirits in such things as trees, rivers and houses. They believe in these spirits most profoundly, and there existence is as real as the physical, visible world. All the tribes believe in 1 god in overall control of the others, and most have taken on board some aspects of the other religions of the region. Buddhist, Tao and Christian symbols have been adopted to some extent by different tribes, and Christian missionaries have obtained many total converts since they began preaching over 40 years ago. Since the missionaries bring with them education and modern medicine, they are having quite a powerful effect in some areas.

Most tribes have 2 types of religious leader. The village priest controls the ritual life of the village, and the shaman has the power to consult directly with the spirit world. The position of priest is usually a hereditary title, but the shaman is selected by various signs that he has the powers of a medium.

KAREN

This tribe is divided into 2 major divistions - Şkaw and Pwo, who have slightly different religious beliefs. Both seek to find harmony between their existence and their gods. Their chief god is the 'Lord of land and water' who owns all the jungle, fields, water and land in the vicinity. Every year, at harvest and new year, and to celebrate all events, and whenever disease or other misfortune strikes the village, at a ceremony led by the oldest woman in the tribe, a sacrifice is made to this god. Chickens are sacrificed, and a pig eaten. After the ceremony, the villagers go home with soil on their ears so as to be invisible to the spirit world.

Recently, many men have adopted extensive tattoos in patterns particular to their sub group. They are thought to bring good luck.

There are many other spirits which must be placated to keep them harmless, and certain spots in the jungle are the home of these spirits. A spirit spring, for example, may cause lameness if trodden in. There are many souls which live within the human body which keep the body alive and well. The loss of 1 of these spirits causes illness, and death results if they all leave. The souls of a child are especially vulnerable, and may be enticed away by the souls of the dead, so Karen children are not allowed even to look at a corpse.

The goddess of the crops - the 'Crop Grandmother' controls the harvest and sits on the stumps of the burnt trees protecting the crop from disease or other calamity. For this reason, damaging or touching the stumps is taboo. The Karen use rice liquor in their ceremonies which must be brewed within the village.

Many of the Karen believe in a prophecy that they will be delivered by a 'messiah' figure who will lead them to a magnificent palace in a great city.

HMONG

The Hmong also believe in a 'Lord of the land' who protects the village from evil. Each village creates a 'spirit shelf' for this deity in a large tree close to the village. During the New Year festivals offerings are made to this spirit.

There are many spirits associated with the home. The main ones are the spirits of the ancestral altar, central post, fireplace, stove, door and bedroom. The spirit of the altar Tzu Kang is the most powerful. The main feature of the altar is a piece of white paper which gives protection to all the occupants of the house. At the New Year festival a cockerel is sacrificed at this altar and feathers stuck to the paper with its blood. If the structure of the house is at risk from storm or flood, the head of the household will call on the spirits for protection.

Most religious rituals are performed by the head of the household (the oldest male), but each village will have one or more shamans to contact the spirit world when necessary. These are chosen by going through a long illness, cured only when the afflicted person consents to be a shaman. During communion with the spirit world he goes into a trance, wearing a black cloth over his eyes to see the spirits. He faces the shamans altar and shakes a ceremonial rattle, sometimes going into violent fits and demanding a sacrifice. After the ceremony, paper money is burned to pay the gods for their sevices.

MIEN

The life of the MIEN (YAO) is influenced strongly by the spirit world, which they fear greatly. They believe that these spirits are stronger than humans, but less clever. The 'water dragon spirits' have an area kept clear for them behind the house to bring good luck. An ancestral altar within the house is dedicated to the ancestors of the family, and spirits live within the stoves which should not be touched by the feet or leaned against. The human body has many souls which during pregnancy move into the embryo from structures within the house. The souls of young children are easily frightened away, possibly even by being photographed. Like some of the other tribes, new born children are not considered human for several days. All Mien know their ancestry over several generations. The Mien are the only hill tribe to have their own written language, and use a book of ancestors which is used to consult their forefathers on important matters. The underlying religion of the Mien is Taoism, as practiced in China 600 years ago. Their rituals are expensive, and much effort goes into amassing sufficient wealth to pay for them. Each village has a Taoist priest and a shaman who contacts the spirit world.

In the life of the Mien, only meticulous observation of the rituals connected with the spirit world can ensure health, wealth and security. Many of the older Mien are concerned lest contact with the outside world should cause their children to lose these beliefs.

LAHU

The Lahu believe in a village spirit - Ghomuntawe-who protects the village. Most prayers are directed to him. Beneath him there a number of spirits capable of doing good or harm. The house spirit Bobar is benevolent unless angered, while nature spirits are neutral or destructive. Many of these spirits may invade an unwary person, and must be exorcised. The village priest is the main religious teacher and mediator between the villagers and their god. The shaman uses a pronged 'spirit fork' to drive out bad spirits causing sickness. Lahu believe that some spirits can send paper or other material into the body of chosen victims, and the shaman will suck or bite the offending substance out. The Lahu pray to their god and the spirits. Red Lahu have a temple, around which long bamboo poles are erected from which white and yellow cloth streamers are hung. Holy days are observed twice a month at full and new moon, when each villager pours water into a large vessel to symbolize the unity of the community. Villagers have their hands washed to cleanse them of all sins since the last holy day. The same evening a communal bowl of rice is eaten, cooked by the priests wife. Three times a year a one day ceremony is held, before the rice planting and at the gathering in of the rice and maize harvest. Every ceremony is followed by enthusiastic dancing. Many of the Lahu have adopted some of the beliefs of Buddhism and Christianity. A third of the Lahu live within Christian communities.

The Red Lahu are the only group to build temples to their Animist spirits. They are always decorated with flags and streamers, both inside and out.

The Akha swing provides the high point of their New Year festivities, held in August or September. For only four days in the year this swing is used, first by the headman and then by all the village inhabitants.

At the gates to every Akha village there will be one or more of these wooden sculptures, symbolising that beyond this point only humans may go

All Akha villages are protected by gates, replaced annually. A typical village will have a series of these gates at its entrance.

AKHA

The Akha have no word for religion - the term 'the Akha way' sums up their spiritual beliefs, and embraces all their activities. Anyone who does not follow the Akha way must leave the tribe.

They worship the spirits of their ancestors, and see themselves as essential links between their forefathers and descendants.

The Akha believe in an all powerful being who is the common ancestor of all Akha people. He taught them to construct an ancestral altar and how to perform offerings to their ancestors. Each house has an altar tied to a roof support, and contains the first three heads of rice cut in the preceding harvest. At new year, rice planting and some other important times, the ancestors are offered a meal of a chicken and some other food items. It is believed that if the ancestors are fed, then they will feed the family with good luck throughout the year.

According to Akha myth, the spirit and human worlds at one time lived together in harmony, but theft of each others property caused so much conflict that the separation of the two worlds was the only solution. To show a clear line between the spirit and human world it was decided that village gates should be constructed at the upper and lower entrance to each village. When entering the village, it is necessary to pass through these gates to cleanse oneself of the spirit powers of the jungle. Male and female carved figures are placed at the gates to indicate entry into the human world. New gates are built each year, so villages are usually entered through a tunnel of old gates. Villages are also characterised by a huge ceremonial swing in a commanding position above the village. Every year there is a 4 day swinging festival, whose religious significance has been forgotten.

Great spirits are those of the sun and moon, and three 'lords' in charge of people, livestock and rice. There is a spirit who lives in swamps and causes malaria and other spirits in trees, rocks, streams and even termite mounds. All these are capable of causing harm if wronged. The spirits of a child who died before being named, and that of a woman who died in childbirth are especially dangerous. The latter may return as a 'weretiger' killing people and livestock.

Most villages are ministered to by a village priest in charge of all religious

To cure minor sicknesses, the Lisu build a bamboo boat in which fragments of the sufferers clothes are placed to 'sail away' the illness.

ceremonies, and a shaman who communicates with the spirit world by going into a trance, and is used to cure illness.

The dog is venerated by the Akha. A soup prepared from a dogs bones is believed to restore strength to the old. To sacrifice a dog is a major event.

LISU

The 'village guardian' controls the village, and is potentially dangerous. There are four other categories of spirits: ancestral, forest, owner and 'bad death' - these are especially dangerous, being the souls of dead people which have not gone to rest but roam the earth and may attack the living. Ancestors are important in family life. They are represented on the house altar by small bowls, and must be fed three times a year. If looked after properly they will ensure good health and crops. Other spirits reside in hills, fields, trees, the sun and moon, etc. The Lisu believe that a person may be possessed by weretigers or vampires. If this is suspected, it is very difficult for anyone in the family to find a marriage partner. The spirit of a weretiger may be present in valuable objects left in the jungle by the possessed, which will cause possession if picked up.

The village priest is particularly powerful to the Lisu, since he is almost an incarnation of the guardian spirit. A shaman contacts the other spirits, and in the case of illness or misfortune sings himself into a trance, and is said to be 'ridden by the spirits' as if he were a horse. A spectacular ceremony is when he sprays alcohol from his mouth over a fire, creating a fireball over the afflicted person. Any male who shows that he has the gift can become a shaman. Indications are that he is physically weak, plays in the fire and does not go to the fields to work. He will go insane if given food forbidden to shamen, only recovering when the correct sacrifice is made. This proof will be followed by an initiation ceremony led by other local shamen, who call down the spirits to 'ride' the new shaman.

The Lisu believe that the spirit of the stream is a frequent cause of sickness, so build many bridges over any water. To discover the cause of sickness, the remains of chickens or pigs bladders are read by an experienced older person.

HOUSE AND VILLAGE

In human evolution it could be said that cooperation between group members was essential for our survival. A hill tribe village is a tightly knit, closely linked group of people who can only succeed and ultimately survive through mutual help and support. The bond between villagers is only slightly less close than that between parents and their children. Hill tribe families live in houses built of bamboo or wooden planks. In most tribes houses are raised above ground level on stilts. The design of houses varies from one tribe to another, but all have one or more fireplaces, a thatched roof and no chimney - consequently they tend to be very smoky inside and partially blackened with soot. All the tribes except the Karens live as extended families, so the houses are large and frequently extended as new family members are born.

Village sites are carefully chosen using astrological and religious signs. The most commonly used test involves the placing of rice grains under a bowl and leaving it for some time. If the grains move, the spirits are registering their disapproval and a new site must be chosen. Villages must be in areas suitable for farming. not too close to other villages and protected from natural dangers.

As the land in the vicinity eventually becomes infertile, village sites must move at intervals. Every ten years is typical, although some Karen villages are over twenty years old. The death of the village priest may be another reason for a move. People are reluctant to move, since the spirits of their children are still attached to their placentas, buried in or around the house.

The size of a village can vary from just two or three houses up to ninety or so. As the populations are rising so rapidly, village populations become too large for the locally available farmland and satellite villages spring up at a suitable radius from the parent village.

House building is a communal activity, although materials will have been collected by the family. The head of the household gives a feast later for all those who have contributed their labour.

The upkeep and supply of communal services is shared between villagers. Paths must be maintained, water sources kept clean and burial grounds tended. If villagers are needed for other duties, such as looking after village guests,Thai soldiers or government officials, the responsibility is passed from family to family.

Corrugated iron rooves are gradually replacing thatch - much less attractive but much more practical.

KAREN

The Karens live in mountain villages, but at lower levels than other tribes, between 600 and 1,000 metres. Villages develop in clusters around the original village. Due to the nature of their agriculture, with fewer cash crops, Karen villages move less frequently than the other tribes. If the village priest dies, then a move used to be mandatory, but only of a few metres to placate the spirits. For this reason permanent crops, such as orchards, can be developed, together with large gardens and tobacco fields. Houses are small and simple, since only husband, wife and unmarried children can live in the same house. Lineages are directed down the female side of the family, other adult women would cause a clash of lineages so families are nuclear rather than extended. Each house is built on stilts and consists of a single large room with screened off areas for adult daughters. Adult unmarried sons should not sleep in the same house as daughters of marriageable age, so must sleep on the verandas of friends. Entry to the house is through a front door leading off a large open veranda and a fireplace, often kept permanently alight, towards the back of the room. Karens are the only people not to have an altar within the house, nor any centres of worship within the village. The only sacred areas are the burial ground and a shrine to the lord of air and water outside the village. The granary is built outside the house, at an angle and below it. Rice pounders are foot operated, one serving several houses. Livestock are kept beneath the house - usually pigs and cattle. Houses should not be arranged in a regular triangular pattern, and branches of the same family should not be next to each other.

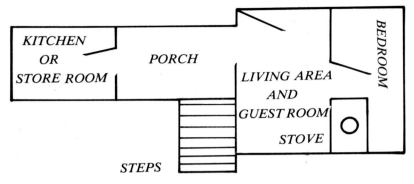

PLAN OF KAREN HOUSE.

Domesticated animals live around and beneath a Pwo Karen's headman's house in this village near Mae Sariang.

HMONG

Most Hmong villages are at high altitudes where opium can be grown most successfully. Usually the village will be in the lee of a hill, protected from wind and monsoon rain. The site must be at a reasonable distance from the fields to prevent damage from domestic animals and there must be a good burial ground within reach. All houses must face downhill and must not be in direct line, as this might prevent the entry of beneficial household spirits. Houses tend to be in clusters around an important persons house. Ceremonial bridges can be seen around the village, connected with healing rites. When a village moves, an advance group will choose a new site and plant crops near that site to provide food for the move of the rest of the village.

Hmong houses are not built on stilts. They are large enough to accommodate the many people of an extended family. The choice of site for a house is subject to the will of the spirits, and paper money is burned to thank the spirits for their help. Houses are built of hardwood planks and thatched with grass or rattan leaves. When the house is completed two chickens are sacrificed at the newly installed altar and the ancestors and household spirits are invited to enter. A rooster and hen are sacrificed at the door to the important door spirits and a wooden sword hung over the door to ward off evil spirits.

A typical Hmong house consists of a large living area with at least one altar, a stove, fireplace, rice pounder, altars and a table. There are one or two doors, two bedrooms, one for parents and one for children and frequently a third bedroom and a guest platform. There is a ladder to an attic in which food, tools and seed are stored. Stables are built against the house for horses and mules, pig sties and granaries are some way away from the house.

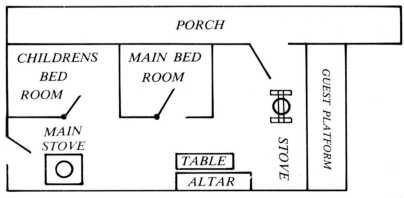

PLAN OF HMONG HOUSE

MIEN (YAO)

Most Mien villages consist of ten to thirty houses built on a slight slope with a nearby water supply. There is no well defined pattern to the arrangement of houses, and no obvious ceremonial or other public areas. Mien houses are built usually of wooden planks on the ground. The roof may be of thatch or wooden slates. There are three entrances; a mens door, leading to the mens side of the house, a womens door leading to the womens side with cooking facilites and a third used for ceremonies. Houses are large, since they must accommodate the sometimes large number of people in an extended family - commonly twenty or more. Within the large living area are three stoves, a main one, one for guests and one for preparing pig food, a table and benches, a rice pounder and the centrally located ancestral altar with perhaps a miniature house upon it. The number of bedrooms depends on the size of the family. Girls of marriagable age have a private bedroom in which they can entertain suitors. An area is kept clear behind the house for the water dragon spirit.

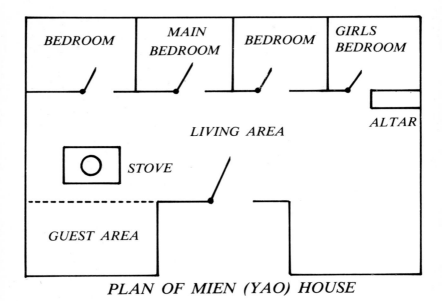

PLAN OF MIEN (YAO) HOUSE

This Lahu village is situated in dramatic mountain scenery typical of the Mae Hong Son area.

In a Lahu village the houses are separated by wicker fences giving a neat, enclosed appearance.

LAHU

Lahu prefer to farm at high altitudes for the production of opium. Villages have a temple or a ritual dance area in a prominent position in the village. There are between fifteen and thirty five houses per village and about six people per house, since the Lahu live as nuclear rather than extended families.

Houses are usually built on stilts with walls of bamboo or wooden planks, thatched with grass. A ladder leads to an open porch with one door to the main room which has a central fireplace. There is one large bedroom, partitioned off as necessary according to family size, and an altar, sometimes enclosed, in one corner.

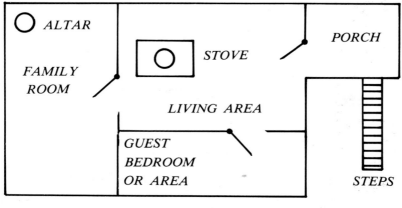

PLAN OF LAHU HOUSE

AKHA

An Akha village should be built on a high ridge with access to drinking water and good arable land. They are typifed from a distance by the huge,high rooves,the enormous wooden ceremonial swing and the series of ceremonial gates at the entrance with their wooden male and female statues. Akha use an 'egg test' to find out if the chosen site is acceptable to the spirits. The priest drops an egg from head height onto a hole in the ground. If the egg does not break, the site is suitable. The priests house is the first to be built, then others are grouped around it - except for the families of 'reject' children, who must live lower down the hill. The Akha live as extended families, so are generally large.

It is not polite to go through an Akha house without stopping for a drink or meal, as it is not polite to pass through a village without stopping at a house. Houses are built on a subframe of wooden posts with bamboo walls and a grass roof. There are no windows, and the eaves outside come down almost to ground level, so the inside of an Akha house is dark, but well protected from cold, wind and rain. Each house has an ancestral altar, the vital centre of the family, situated in the corner of the womans section. There are two or three fireplaces, one for cooking meat, the other for vegetables. The third is used for cooking the pigs food.

69

Akha houses are built at ground level. The scalloped ridges give them a distinctive style. This headmans house is just north of the Kok river near Chiang Rai.

Akha villages are always situated at high altitudes close to a mountain ridge, often giving dramatic views to the valleys below.

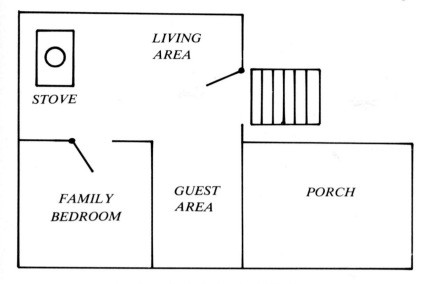

PLAN OF AKHA HOUSE

LISU

Many Lisu are semi dependent on the sale of opium for their survival. Villages are built between the opium fields at about 1600 metres and their crops at 1000 metres. Ideally they should be close to, but not in contact with, a good supply of water, as they are afraid of the water spirits. They need to be fairly near another community which can sell them crops in lean years, their money coming from opium sold to Yunnanese traders.

When a suitable site has been found, they perform a ceremony in which the spirits are asked for their approval of the site using the rice grain test mentioned earlier.

Central to each village is a fenced off shrine to the guardian spirit, a place of communal worship and sacrifice. Any family moving into or out of the village must make a sacrifice to the shrine, as must the parents of new born babies.

Lisu house and village

Houses may be on the ground or on stilts. They are made of bamboo poles around a central ridge. The main bedroom is on the uphill side, next to the ancestral altar, with large families the number of bedrooms will be increased as necessary. Girls after puberty have a bedroom of their own. Guests sleep on a guest platform in a corner of the large living area. They must not interfere with the altar or sleep with their heads towards the fire and must not enter the bedrooms.

On completion of a house the altar is installed and the household spirits invited to take up residence with the sacrifice of two cocks and a hen Meat from them is put on the altar to persuade the household spirits to stay.

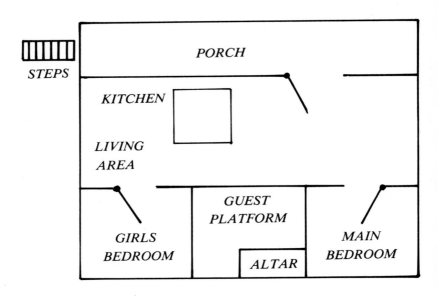

PLAN OF LISU HOUSE

BIRTH AND MARRIAGE

Birth is the most dangerous time of life for all hill tribe people. Amongst women complications in childbirth are the commonest forms of death, and infant mortality, especially at the time of birth, is very high. The average number of children born is close to six to each couple, partly to offset infant mortality. Children are insurance against sickness and old age, so it is vital to have enough to ensure that some survive. Death rates have been falling over the last 30 years, with a gradual increase in wealth from cash crops and the introduction of western medicine, so the high birth rate coupled with a falling death rate is the major cause of the rapid increase in the populations of the hill tribes.

Because of the dangers, pregnancy and birth are surrounded by ritual and taboo. The woman usually gives birth in a squatting position, the baby landing on the bamboo or dirt floor. She is generally helped by a relative or specialised midwife.

For most hill tribes the baby is not considered a human being until it has lived for a few days - the soul that enters the embryo is fragile and easily frightened away. The mothers diet and behaviour during pregnancy and after the birth of the baby are carefully regulated. For most hill tribes, death of the mother in childbirth is a 'bad death', and likely to result in her spirit returning to haunt the village.

Courtship varies greatly from tribe to tribe. Most have a high degree of etiquette, lineages must be carefully consulted and good omens looked for before permission to marry can be given. Monogamy is usual, although some tribesmen may take a second wife. The marriage ceremony is always a great celebration, and usually very expensive for the bride or grooms family. Since the couple frequently come from different villages, the occasion provides a rare opportunity for young people to meet new friends, and one marriage frequently spawns others !

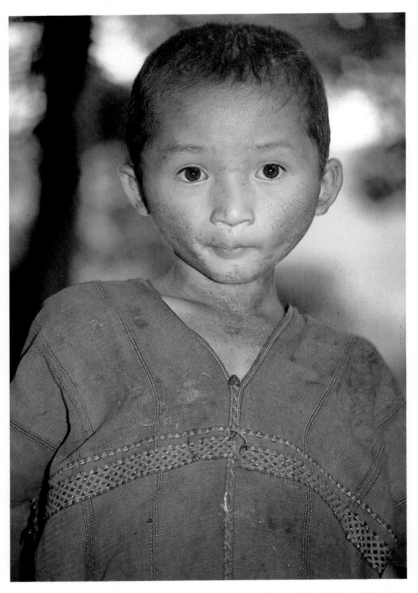

This rather wistful Pwo Karen boy is wearing the traditional shirt of his tribe.

KAREN

When a Karen woman is pregnant she must not drink alcohol or certain foods which might cause a miscarriage. If a tree is felled across her path, the person responsible must make her a gift of a chicken, or a problem in childbirth may result. She must not see a corpse or a coffin, as the soul of the unborn baby may be lured away to the underworld.

A Karen women usually gives birth in her own home, assisted by her husband or other close relative. A midwife (male or female) may be used in a difficult birth, coupled with spells and perhaps the sacrifice of a suitable animal. The umbilical cord is cut with a sliver of bamboo, and the placenta is placed in a bamboo tube which may be hung out side the village or buried under the veranda.

After the birth, the mother stays by the fire for three days, sitting upright to prevent blood flowing to her head. She will usually eat only rice and chicken. The day after birth the father ties a thread of white cotton around his wifes neck to relieve worry, and during early childhood the childs ears are pierced to show to the spirits that it is not a monkey. At this ceremony, the baby becomes officially human. To protect the baby from illness, amulets are tied around its neck. If the baby is ill when over 2 weeks old, the parents must 'buy back' its soul by sacrificing a chicken.

Courtship can be frustrating for young Karens, since unmarried couples should not meet in private. There are opportunities to meet at communal planting, weeding and harvesting, but courtship takes place at funerals. Karen girls are not supposed to give any signs of interest in a suitor, and are generally reserved and unsmiling, although it is not unusual for girls to propose marriage. Marriage between rather than within villages is encouraged, and in the dry season young men may visit other villages to find prospective wives.

The wedding lasts two or three days. The bride to be will have woven a shirt for her husband, who arrives in old clothes until presented with her gift. His mother in law sprinkles his feet with water, cleansing him of spirits. The bride then washes the grooms hands, and the couple then eat a hen and cockerel cooked together. The bride changes from her one piece spinster dress into her more colourful two piece dress.

Karen

The couple live together in the bride's village, if possible, but recently whichever village has the better land is chosen.

Pre marital sex is prohibited, and a fine is imposed if it is known to have happened. It happens. Divorce and adultery are rare. An offending adulterous couple must make a large sacrifice and are driven from the village.

A Skaw Karen extended family. Generally the children too young to work in the fields will be cared for by their grandparents.

A Blue Hmong infant from a village south of Mae Hong Son. Although often comparatively rich, Hmong families cling tenaciously to traditional dress and customs.

Hill tribe men rarely wear traditional costume, but this Blue Hmong father reveals the very beautiful colours and patterns worn by his tribe.

HMONG

To the Hmong, babies are sent into this world by a 'baby goddess' and belong to the spirit world for the first 3 days of their lives. On the third day a ceremony is held to witness the babies soul taking up residence and to make a sacrifice of thanks to the 'baby goddess'.

Only the husband or midwife can assist at the birth. The mother sits between 2 stools to give birth. The placenta is buried outside the bedroom door. The mother lies by the fire for three weeks, eating only chicken and rice, before resuming a normal life.

Courtship is highly ritualised. At the 3 day New Year festival, boys and girls of the right age line up opposite each other. Each girl has a black ball which she throws to the partner of her choice. He then has the choice to accept her invitation or not. Pre marital sex is common, boys taking a red blanket to the house of his prospective mate to tempt her to join him inside it. Commonly Hmong boys will go to another village to find a mate.

Once parents have given permission for a couple to marry, much haggling may be necessary to determine the 'bride price'. Generally about 10,000 baht in silver. During this time the couple will have been living together. Once the price has been decided, it may be months or years before the groom's family can pay and the wedding can take place. The bride's mother may make a great show of pretending to get her daughter back, even beating her future son-in-law with sticks !

When the bride price has been paid in full, the bride becomes the property of her husband and his family, and if she later wants to leave must pay the bride price back to her husband's family. If she wants to marry again, she must pay 2,000 baht to her first husband.

The wedding festival starts at the groom's house, who must provide pigs, chickens and alcohol. The groom bows to all the relatives in turn, in order of seniority, and to the household and ancestral spirits.

It is not uncommon for better off Hmong men to take two or more wives. Each time a bride price must be paid, unless the man marries the widow of an elder brother.

MIEN (YAO) mothers put all their skill into the embroidery of their childrens hat's, which are dramatically colourful and wonderfully made.

MIEN (YAO) children form close bonds with their grandmothers, who traditionally care for them while their mothers work in the fields.

MIEN (YAO)

During pregnancy the soul of a Mien unborn baby lives in various places in the house depending on the month of the year.There are many precautions needed to prevent miscarriage and deformity. Water must not be poured on the fireplace, and the door or rice pounder must not be struck with a knife.

Women give birth at home, but if unmarried must go to a hut outside, and make a chicken sacrifice to be allowed to return. The grandmother-to-be helps at the birth, after which the mother rests for three days by the fire. For a month she must not enter other houses or do any heavy work. A door is cut into her bedroom so she will not pass through any of the other doors until after the cleansing ceremony.

Mien young people have free choice of partner as long as they are of different clans and their birth dates are compatible. Commonly partners will have been living together for some time before they get married, although this practice is dying out, and may already have several children. The bride price and the costs of the wedding are all paid by the groom's family, agreed and subject to a signed contract by both families. Children born before the wedding belong to the bride, afterwards they belong to the groom. During the betrothal period the bride embroiders elaborate wedding clothes for herself and the groom.

The day before the wedding, the bride's family and friends walk to the groom's village. All those who have been invited will have received a small packet of salt. The bride wears an elaborate head piece, and spends the night in the groom's village. The bride price is paid to the bride's father before witnesses. The next morning the priest tells the spirits that a new person is coming to live in the village and purifies the house before the entry of the bride, who arrives with an orchestra. She remains in the bridal chamber until evening, while the guests feast and drink. In the evening the couple are married, then bow three times to all the guests and officials. The next morning there is a final feast after which the bride removes her head dress and is considered a member of her new village.

This Lahu mother and child show the serenity of motherhood found throughout all societies.

An Akha infant eats in comfort whilst his mother carries on with her daily chores.

LAHU

In pregnancy, Lahu women may eat a type of clay which contains some important minerals. During childbirth she kneels on a mat and supports herself with a rope. An older woman usually helps with the birth. The baby drops on the mat and the umbilical cord is cut and tied with a black or white thread - red thread used in ceremonies cannot be used in case the babies soul is tempted away. The placenta is buried beneath the home and protected from animal damage. If there are problems during birth a spirit priest will be called to protect mother and baby. The mother eats only rice and chicken for 12 days after the birth. The new born is named on the first holy day following its birth, if it cries the parents try a new name. Courtship usually takes place at the New Year Good Luck and Harvest festivals. Boys from a village will group together and visit other villages for the purpose of finding a bride. Girls feed the boys and may then pair off. Black Lahu girls are rather forward in chasing and enticing the man of their choice, signalling with torches to their chosen mate. and pre marital sex is usual. Go betweens are used, chosen by the boys, to arrange the marriage. This will be several years away, but after a betrothal ceremony the couple may live together with the girls family. The boy will have to work for a while for his future wifes family before they become officially married after their marriage feast. The Red Lahu wedding feast takes place after the family has collected enough pigs, rice and other food and drink to feast the whole village and the grooms retinue from his village.

The early years of betrothal and marriage are a trial period, and separation and divorce are common. If the boy turns out to be lazy or unpleasant, or if he is homesick and resents working for his wifes family, he will return home. If he wants to leave he must pay a fine and loses any children who remain with the mothers family.

An Akha couple take pride in showing off their traditional costumes.

AKHA

Akha women must observe many taboos during pregnancy, although they try to work until the delivery of the baby. Death in childbirth is a great disaster, involving difficult ceremonies and sacrifices to prevent the return of the mothers soul. Any birth defects in the new born are regarded with horror, as they are believed to disrupt the natural order of things, and are the result of some sin on the part of the parents. Included amongst these defects are all physical oddities like extra fingers or toes, and twins. All these 'rejects' are suffocated at birth and buried far away, after which the whole village must be purified.

Young people are free to marry the person of their choice. Couples meet in the dry season, when boys in small groups may visit other villages. Each village has a 'courting ground' where the girls sing and dance for the boys,and the boys play their gourd pipes,singing and dancing for the girls. Couples may sit together on strategically placed benches,later perhaps going off into the jungle in pairs. Boys will be wearing ceremonial courting jackets and bags with silver ornaments on their turbans. Girls/are supposed to be coy, and refuse when the boys father or elder brother approaches her family on his behalf. When she eventually consents, each father contributes an agreed amount of money held by a neutral party to ensure the two families will honour the contract. After the marriage, the money is returned to the families.

The wedding takes place in the grooms village after the grooms family have collected enough materials for the feast. The brides family cannot attend. The ceremony is presided over by an elderly woman. The bride is married in a white skirt, and carries a lock of her hair which she later drops, symbolising her leaving her old village and joining a new one. An egg is cooked and passed three times between the couple before being eaten by them, this is the moment when they become man and wife. They have mud and dung thrown at them by the guests at the end of the week to initiate them into married life ! The wedding feast lasts two or three days, men and women eating separately. The couple are daubed with soot and pelted with cooked rice to symbolise years of plenty and many children. During or after the feasting the couple receive a long lecture on living life the Akha way. Finally all the elders of the village are honoured.

87

Divorce is common in the early years of the marriage. This may be caused by the wifes adultery, by her inability to have male children, or drug addiction on the part of the husband. The first two children belong to the husbands village. A husband must pay for divorcing his wife, unless she has committed adultery. An Akha man may take a second wife, although this is not common.

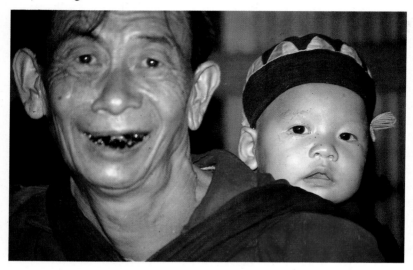

In Lisu culture, it is most often the grandfather who lands the job of caring for the children.

LISU

A Lisu women will give birth close to the fireplace in her home, helped by one or more village women. If labour is difficult offerings may be made to the bad death spirits. She must not drink cold water and must be kept very warm. After birth the mother lies by a fire for one month. After one day sacrifices are made to the village guardian spirit. The baby is given a temporary name after 3 days - until that time it is not regarded as a human being.

Courtship is informal amongst the Lisu - during communal planting or weeding ceremonies, around the rice pounder, in the evenings etc. Girls

This Lisu girl, at ten years old, is not far away from married life.

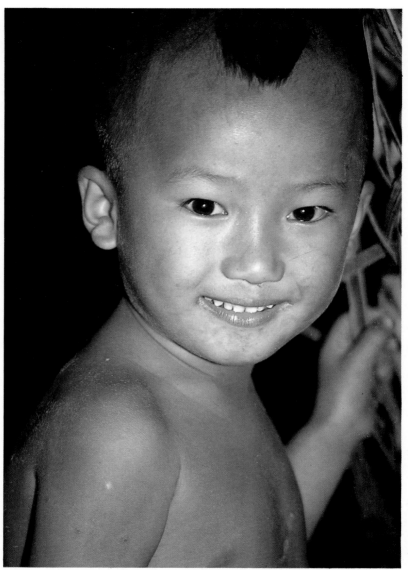

Young Lisu boys have their heads shaved apart from the fontanelle area, since it is believed the spirit can escape through this juvenile gap in the skull.

and boys may form teams and have singing competitions - whichever team cannot remember the next verse of a very long song is the loser. The marriage process is in the form of a stylised drama. The prospective groom gives a money gift to the girl who 'elopes' secretly with him into a jungle hut. A go-between then reassures the girls father that she has not been taken by a tiger, but by her future husband. He refuses to believe this, and later in the day the go-between returns with alcohol and tea and tries to establish a bride price. After much denial, the girls father finally accepts the inevitable, and demands two pieces of cloth and a down payment on the bride. The go-between returns saying it is not possible to raise this money, at which the father also demands money for the girls mother. This scrupulously polite process continues until the bride price is established. The couple will live together until the full bride price has been paid, only being truly married after the marriage ceremony.

The couple are married in front of the ancestral altar in the girls house. The groom bangs his head on the ground three times before his parents in law, the couple are blessed and they share water and rice. There is then a feast, at which guests drop money into a bowl of water. At the end of the feast, the bowl is poured into the grooms hands. He presents the money to his bride. This is 'seed' money, ensuring healthy children for the new couple.

SICKNESS AND DEATH

Hill tribe people value health above all other attributes, as do we all, but the hold of the hill tribesman on his health is rather more tenuous than ours. Their life expectancy is very low, due to poor sanitation, remoteness from medical services, polluted water supplies and a lack of knowledge of hygiene and health. Health is therefore never taken for granted, but has to be worked at.

Sickness is regarded as the will of the spirit world, caused by some sin or insult to the gods. Death is a transition between this world and a parallel spirit world, which is opposite to ours. For example, the people of the spirit world work during the night. The death ceremony is essential to prevent the soul of the departed returning to take more souls to the underworld, and various strategies must be invoked to trick the newly dead spirit to leave the village and not return.

The sick hill tribe person has a number of options. If all ill health is caused by angering a spirit, then the first move is to placate this spirit with sacrifice and the use of a shaman. This may be followed by the use of herbs and local drugs - the commonest used is opium for its analgesic, anti diarrhoea and anti irritant properties, with the risk of consequent addiction.

If these two traditional methods fail to work, the patient may resort to the use of an 'injection doctor' - Thai or Yunnanese, usually untrained but equipped with various western drugs and syringes. Their use may be dangerous, since the diagnosis may be incorrect, or the drug used wrongly, but 'injection doctors' are often more available than the hill tribes last resort - western medicine. This will usually involve a long walk to the nearest hospital or clinic, and frequently the patient may be beyond medical help by the time he or she arrives. Gradually, western medicine is gaining the respect and trust of the hill tribes, whilst the old rituals are maintained.

KAREN

To find the spiritual cause of a disease, the Karen use divination with chicken bones, feathers or grains of rice. A shaman will only be used

92

for a complex case. If an evil spirit is found, the shaman will lure it into a basket which is taken into the jungle and lost.

The Karen believe in heaven and hell - the lowest hell for those who offend the Karen code of honour. The lord of the dead decides the dead persons fate. The spirit world exactly mirrors this one - spirits must work in the fields, eat, sleep etc.

A dead person is washed by their relatives and dressed in their best clothes, except for an unmarried girl who is dressed as a married woman, to prevent an evil spirit taking possession of her. The deceased have songs sung in their honour by young men and women, the women wearing singing shawls and covering their faces with veils while walking around the coffin. The body may be buried or cremated. The funeral rites are to prevent the dead returning to haunt the village, and on their way back from the funeral obstacles are placed in the way of any spirits trying to return.

HMONG

Curing rites are passed from generation to generation amongst the Hmong. In each village there may be several such people-not shamans or priests, but capable of finding the cause of a disease, the relevent spirit and remedy. A common cure attempted for serious illness is the bridge ceremony, in which the patient makes a sacrifice and has a bridge made over a stream or on a path. The sick person is led over the bridge and has strings tied around his wrist. If this does not work, metal neck rings, bracelets or anklets will be tried. If these methods fail, western medicinal techniques may be used.

A sumptuous and expensive funeral is important, since it paves the way to a rich and successful afterlife. It is better to die at home, an event signalled by the firing of a gun and the wailing of family members. The children and grandchildren wash the body, which is then dressed in special burial clothing of several layers of garments richly embroidered, strips of white cloth round the legs and special shoes. Under the head funeral pillows are placed and the fingers are tied with red thread. A red cloth is placed over the face to prevent the corpse from being embarrassed.

A chicken is sacrificed and placed in the coffin above the head. This confirms to the dead person that they are dead.

At the funeral a ceremonial death drum and Hmong mouth organ are played, and the corpse is fed before the coffin is closed and the procession to the burial ground begins. The coffin is lowered into the ground and the carrying poles broken into two so that they will not return to the village and cause the death of others.

MIEN (YAO)

Disease is caused by the loss of one or more of the many souls which dwell in the human body. Traditionally, a shaman is used to cure disease. He will first need to become possessed by his mentor spirit, who will question for him all the immediate ancestors of the family. Using his divining rods, he may have to look further afield in the spirit world until he finds the offended spirit. The tiger spirit is a common cause of illness. He asks this spirit which sacrifice he would prefer and at what date and time the cure will be effected. Paper money is then burned to pay the spirit for his services.

If this fails, a bridge ceremony may be tried. A plank freshly cut from a tree is placed over a stream or beside the path, the more serious the illness, the larger the bridge. The shaman writes letters to the spirit gods and ancestors, then throws rice at the patient across the bridge who catches it and brings it over the bridge. The shaman presents the patient with a live chicken and a rod. The patient now walks back over the bridge to his village, without looking back, from the chicken on one side to a pig on the other - both sacrifices, and the missing soul will return to restore health. If the patient cannot walk, his clothing is carried over.

The funeral service lasts three days and is complex. The dying persons head is lifted three times by each of their children to ease their passing. At death, the eyes are closed and a silver coin placed in the dead persons mouth to prevent the dead person telling lies. Relatives wash the body and cut its hair. The body is clothed and placed on a shelf before the ancestral altar. The family collect the items needed for the funeral. These include paper money, pigs for sacrifice, rice and alcohol.

A priest is put in charge, and orders six men to make the coffin. On completion, he sprinkles it with holy water to drive out spirits from the wood. There follow many prayers. Relatives and guests wear white cloths on their heads as a mark of respect. The soul forces of the deceased are driven from the body, appearing as pieces of white paper on the foot of the priest. Coming away from the coffin is a blue cloth which leads through the roof to a bamboo pole. The souls of the deceased leave the body along this cloth bridge.

The coffin and body are usually buried, unless the person had a bad death, in which case the body is burned on a funeral pyre.

The eldest son stays with the body 7 days, then the priest will return to find some bones of the deceased which are placed in a jar and buried in a spot decided by the egg test.Chronically sick people may move their fathers grave since the cause of the sickness is believed to be the poor siting of a grave.

LAHU

The Lahu do not blame all sickness on the spirits. Only if there is no obvious cause will a supernatural agent be suspected. The Lahu value health very highly, and pray for it daily when taking water to the temple. They may use a Yunnanese or Thai injection doctor, but also stock and use western drugs themselves. Blessing or merit ceremonies are commonly used to offset disease. In these, good deeds such as feeding the hungry will cause the gods to effect a cure. Offerings may be made in the temple, the priest burning candles on the metal 'spirit fork' and praying for the health of the patient. When a man is near death it is said his dog begins to howl, and a bird called the spirit bird begins to sing.

When dead, the body is wrapped in a white sheet and placed in the main room of the house. Food is served to it until it is buried, but at each meal the corpse is reminded that it is leaving soon. The leg and wing of a chicken are placed in the coffin with the corpse. Most Lahu bury their dead, but some use cremation. The body chooses its burial place. An egg is thrown in various directions, the place at which the egg breaks being the chosen spot. After burial, precautions are taken to prevent the return of the spirit to the village. Thorny branches are placed alongside the path back from the burial ground which the villagers brush against to remove any evilness. They bring back branches from near the grave which are dipped in water. All the mourners are sprinkled with water from these branches to purify them. Twelve days after death, the family build a hut for the deceased near the house and furnish it with clothes and a sacrificed chicken. This is to prevent the spirit of the dead person coming any nearer the village, and a prayer is said to persuade it to remain in the 'country of the dead..Relatives of the deceased may stay near the grave for a few days to scare off any weretigers, believed to be a common cause of misfortune and death.

AKHA

Akha believe that if 'the Akha way' is followed exactly, ill health will not occur, although they accept that most physical accidents are not supernaturally caused, and use western medicine, if available, to cure these.

Disease caused by wronging a spirit are called 'spirit afflictions'. If the spirit that has been wronged can be discovered, and the wrong put right, then the patient will recover.

The bones of animals killed by lightning, or 'lightning bolts' (stone age axe heads) are used in curing ceremonies.'Soul loss' is a common cause of affliction and disease. To treat this the soul must be called back in a ceremony. Afterwards, strings are tied around the patients wrist to prevent any of his souls leaving again. The roots and bark of various trees are used as cures. The Akha recognize that many diseases are hereditary. Anyone from an affected family will find it difficult to find a marriage partner.

After death, the body is washed and pieces of gold are put in the mouth of the corpse, so that it can buy whatever is necessary in the next world. The body is wrapped in a black shroud and covered in a red cloth. Until burial, a wake is held, with singing, gambling and ceremonies.

The coffin is a beautifully designed structure resembling a boat. The body is placed inside and the family pay their last respects by brushing the eyes of the deceased with cotton. Several sets of clothes are placed on the body before the coffin is tightly sealed. Burial takes place usually a few days later. A spirit priest chants the Akha death rites for two days, giving the corpse precise instructions on how to reach the spirit world. The grave is dug in an east - west orientation, and personal possessions left on the grave. A bag of food parcels is left on a stick above the grave. Final rites allow the corpse to converse with its spirit ancestors, and keep off weretigers. The family then have a 'meal of separation' to show the corpse that it must not return. A year later the spirit is invited back to watch over the household.

If a man dies leaving no heir, the body must be taken out through a hole in the wall and the altar of the house must be destroyed, since no-one now has the right to use it.

Following a 'bad death' a purification ceremony must be held before the burial. A dog must be buried over the coffin to prevent the spirit calling out.

The Akha regard death as taboo, and it is never talked about except at the appropriate time.

LISU

The Lisu believe that evil spirits and loss of soul cause sickness. To find the offending spirit, an expert is consulted who will 'read' the liver of a sacrificed pig or the thigh bones of a chicken. In serious cases a shaman will be consulted who must 'ride' the spirits. Often several spirits are involved, each one demanding a sacrifice. Many pigs and chickens may be needed to placate the spirits, so illness may be very expensive-although the sacrificed animals are eaten by the people of the village.

To call back a soul that has left someone, 'bridges' must be built-planks of wood alongside a path festooned with streamers. The patient sits before his family altar while the priest slowly returns from the bridge, enticing the spirit to return, finally tying cords around the neck of the patient. Illness may also be caused by a person or spirit sending objects into the body of the sufferer which must be sucked out quickly, or death will result. Sharp, stabbing pains are diagnosed in this way, and shamans may claim to be able to send the object into the body of the person or spirit responsible.

Death is believed to be pre ordained by the god Yelaun. In his book , The individuals life span is noted. At the point of death, grains of rice and pieces of silver are placed in the mouth. A gun is fired to announce the death. The corpse is washed and a coffin made. That night, a death song is sung urging the spirit of the deceased not to return. Until burial, a wake is held, with feasting, drinking, singing and gambling to prevent the relatives feeling too sad. At the graveyard, the egg test is used to find the correct spot for burial. Above the grave, a basket is hung containing rice, cloth, water and a knife. The water is changed daily for ten days. The poles used to carry the coffin are broken and laid on top of the grave to prevent the spirit returning to the village. The burial party splash water on the path and on the mourners for purification, and to prevent the return of the soul of the deceased.

Back in the village, a shot is fired. Later, a shaman performs a ceremony in which the extended family of the deceased have a long chord wrapped around them. He sprays them with water as a final protection against the return of the deceased. A month later the bowl of water by the grave is returned and placed on the family altar to show that the spirit of the deceased has become an honoured ancestor. Every year for three years the family will sacrifice a pig and two chickens and prayers are said both to the deceased and to the 'lord of the graves'.

AGRICULTURE AND ECONOMY

The hilltribes have what is termed a subsistence economy. They grow enough food for their own consumption and hopefully enough excess to exchange, barter or sell to provide themselves with clothing, tools, weapons, ornaments and other necessary or desired items.

Land is not owned, so there is no separation into landed and landless classes. The only limitation on how much land can be used by each family is their ability to clear, plant and weed their area. Some families will be more successful than others, however, and become wealthier and have higher status, but this is likely to be a temporary situation. In poor years, members of some families will be forced by economic necessity to become hired labourers for other tribes or for Thai farmers, and as the hill tribe population increases and the fertility of the land declines this is becoming more common, with all its dangers of diluting the integrity of the tribes.

The maintainance of status is a vital part of hill tribe life. For the Karens, status comes from owning elephants. In the other tribes, the number and size of sacrifices, the magnificence of wedding and funeral feasts and the amount of jewellery worn by the family determine ones standing in the community. This mutual sharing has a cohesive function, maintaining the links between families and a group identity, rather like buying rounds of drinks in a bar. Since the protein consumed at feasts and some sacrifices is consumed by the whole village, this is an important means of distributing wealth and preventing protein deficiency diseases in the poorer families.

Livestock are an important status symbol. They are kept in the village, either beneath the houses or in separate stables. Pigs, cattle, water buffalo, chickens, cats and dogs are found in all the hilltribes, elephants amongst the Karens. In addition to being a source of protein, pigs and chickens have great ceremonial importance. They are killed and eaten to mark special occasions - at times of birth, marriage, death or as a sacrifice. Cattle are highly prized. They are easy to keep, tended usually by small boys, and can be easily sold for cash when needed. Some tribal people look after cattle for lowlanders, receiving any calves produced in payment. Water buffalo are needed for ploughing irrigated rice paddies, and may be owned or rented for the required period. The Akha sacrifice water buffalo at the funeral of important villagers.

Ponies and oxen are used as pack animals for transporting goods to the villages. Ponies in particular are highly prized.

Hunting and fishing provide another source of protein, although very little game is still found in the hills. Sambur and barking deer, monkeys, squirrels, birds, snakes and lizards are trapped or shot with gun and crossbow. Fungii, bamboo shoots, honey, various roots and tubers and edible insects supplement the hilltribe diet.

As money becomes a more important part of the economy, there has been a shift away from the growing of crops for consumption within the village to the production of cash crops - crops grown primarily to sell or exchange. Foremost amongst these is opium, as it is easy to grow, is collected by traders who travel to the villages and is profitable. The trade is controlled largely by the Yunnanese who pay low prices to the hilltribes, who are not in a position to argue since the crop is illegal. The Thai government is sponsoring the hilltribes to grow other crops, such as coffee. With some success. Tea is the second major cash crop, controlled largely by Thai traders in Chiang Mai and other towns who supply the means of transport from the hills and a constant market. The tea leaves are popular amongst Thais, chewed with salt as a stimulant.

TYPES OF AGRICULTURE

1. Swidden (slash and burn)

Swidden is an old English word meaning literally 'a burned clearing in the forest', but now tends to be used to describe any pattern of shifting agriculture. It involves the burning of natural vegetation, growing crops on the burned land for a few seasons, then waiting for the natural vegetation to regenerate.

At tropical temperatures there is a very rapid recycling of nutrients, so that at any given time most of these will be in the vegetation. When the vegetation is cut down and burned, the ash will contain these nutrients and support a crop shallow rooted enough to use them. Burning also kills most of the pests and diseases present in the soil. At each harvest the nutrients are taken away with the crop, so the soil is quickly exhausted, and the land must be left for several years. During this time nutrients will build up again through recolonisation by wild plants, so that after some time the land can be used again.

Swidden agriculture is associated with tropical climates with a dry season in which vegetation can be successfully burned. Only a few simple hand tools are needed, and there is no attempt to improve the land by the use of fertilizers or ploughing. It can support only a low density of population, since much of the land must be left to regenerate, and there is no ownership of the land.

This system can be maintained indefinately with no damage to the environment if the population remains low and at a low density, but it can be extremely damaging if it is abused. Hill tribe populations are expanding very rapidly - doubling every twenty years, and in many areas land is no longer left long enough to regenerate properly. There is no doubt that given these conditions, traditional swidden agriculture must change before the hills of Northern Thailand are turned into a desert. There are several types of swidden agriculture which show variations between the tribes.

Rotating field system

This is practiced by the Karen and Lahu. It is suited to steep hillsides where there is water available for irrigation.Houses are grouped in small hamlets, related in size to the amount of available land within a reasonable walking distance. The headman allocates the swiddens amongst the families according to their needs, and each swidden is farmed on a strict rotation. If the land is very fertile, a swidden can be used every four years. Poor land may need to lie fallow for twenty years. The trees must reach a height of about four metres before they can be burned again. Some trees will be left within each swidden, probably to reseed the area quickly after the crop has been taken.

Firing the swidden before planting is carefully controlled, with fire breaks around the edge. Rarely is any forest outside the swidden fire damaged - all the men in the village are employed in preventing this at the time of firing.

Dry rice cultivation in Pwo Karen field. Corn and rice are grown together. The trees are beginning to regenerate.

The soil is not disturbed before planting, thus preventing soil erosion. Seeds are dropped into small holes made in the ash. During the wet season weeding is carried out, the uprooted weeds are laid on the soil surface to cover it and thus stop other weeds invading. To prevent erosion, ditches are dug parallel to the slope.

To sum up, this method of farming allows semi permanent occupation of an area, and if carried out carefully has no detrimental environmental effect.

Non cyclic swiddens

These are used for the production of rice, corn and poppy. There is no attempt to re-use swiddens once they have become infertile. After a few years, when the soil has been denuded of nutrients, a new area of forest is burned. Villages are moved frequently as the need for new land arises, so the community does not feel so emotionally attached to their land. Usually, corn and poppy are grown together in one swidden and the other is used exclusively for rice. Rice swiddens do not normally last for more than two years, but corn and poppy can be grown for up to ten years in the same swiddens. Corn is useful in that it discourages weeds, but has the disadvantage that it takes up a lot of the available nutrients. Poppies must be grown at high elevations, rice must be below 1000 metres, corn will grow anywhere.

Swiddens are prepared towards the end of the dry season, usually in March. Corn is planted in May, and rice immediately afterwards. Poppy seeds are planted in September or October after the corn is harvested. Rice is harvested in November and December and the opium collected in February or March.

The growing of poppies tends to be damaging to the environment. Soil structure is disturbed by the preparation of a fine topsoil necessary for germination. Swiddens are burned every year after crop collection to kill weeds, and burning is not carefully carried out. When the village moves the soil is almost devoid of nutrients and only poor grasses can recolonise. It is many years before the land can recover.

Wet rice cultivation near a Karen village. Although by far the most productive farming type, it is rarely available to the hill tribes.

Irrigated fields

Land must be level, and can be used continuously since irrigation provides nutrients to replace those lost when the harvest is taken. A mud wall is built to hold back the water and maintain it at the best level. The source of water can either be rainwater or taken by canal and ditch from a stream or river. The latter is much preferable as crops can be grown throughout the year rather than just in the rainy season.

The main crop grown is flood irrigated rice. After this has been harvested other crops less dependent on continuous water can be grown, such as garlic, corn and tobacco.

Irrigated fields provide the richest and most reliable farmland. They are the basis of the lowland Thai agricultural system, but are in short supply in the hills. Most hilltribe villages do not have access to them, and since they are owned and have a market value they do not fit well with the culture of the hill tribes. They are, however, highly desired by all the villages.

Orchards and gardens

This term covers all agricultural land permanently cultivated but not flood irrigated. Some hilltribe villages, especially amongst the Karens, will have tea, mango , lemon, jackfruit, longon, lime, pineapple, sugar cane or lychee orchards. Wild tea trees occur naturally in many areas of Northern Thailand, and management is usually restricted to the felling of competing trees. Cotton, tobacco and vegetables are typical wet season crops.

In recent years many flood irrigated fields have been replaced with longon orchards. This has been caused by the original hill tribe farmers getting into debt and selling their valuable irrigated fields to local merchants who can afford to wait the several years necessary to extract a highly profitable longon crop.

A small but increasing contribution to the hilltribe economy comes from tourism. Tour guides pay for the use of services, food and accommodation for tourists, a small amount, but in villages on the main trekking routes a useful additional income. The sale of handicrafts, either directly to visiting groups or from such outlets as the street markets in the larger towns, also provides much needed cash for the villages.

Periodic visits to the nearest market town are now normal for tribal men. They take with them handicrafts, charcoal, thatch shingles and other jungle produce which they sell in exchange for clothing (it is now usual to see hill ltribe people in a mixture of traditional clothing and western T shirts, and shorts) salt, iron, medicines, cloth, torches, batteries, sewing equipment and other household goods.

If visits to market are difficult, another source of supply of these goods are Yunnanese traders, who travel through the hilltribe area selling goods which they know are popular. Prices are high due to the risks these traders take, from bandits and other sources. Tribal men commonly use the slack agricultural period for trading. Livestock are bought in one village and sold at a profit, either in another village or at market.

The traditional independence of the hilltribes is disappearing as they are coming to rely more and more heavily on selling their labour. Poor Karens commonly work for Hmong and Lisu, while poor Lahu and Akha work on the opium fields of Mien (Yao), Lisu and Yunnanese. Many tribes people hire themselves out to lowland Thai farmers as agricultural workers. Payment is often in rice.

Large debts are becoming increasingly common, as villagers have to buy rice and other essentials on credit. Eventually, desperate tribespeople are forced to sell their crops in advance, or even their daughters who may end up in brothels elsewhere in Thailand.

The economic future for the hilltribes looks bleak. Traditional farming methods are becoming impossible to maintain with an expanding population, and the alternatives will inevitably damage or destroy the long term integrity of the hilltribe cultures. Poverty and malnutrition are increasing, and despite the good efforts of the Thai government agencies it is difficult to be optimistic about the future.

A Hilltribe Day

The women rise about half an hour before dawn and prepare a fire, and cook tea, rice and chillies. The family eat together quickly, then prepare to go to the fields. Old people stay in the village and look after the sick and young children who cannot work. At noon, work stops for half an hour for a packed lunch. The family returns from the fields just before dusk, the women prepare a fire and the evening meal of rice and chillies and perhaps a little meat. The men may hunt for small game for an hour or so. After dinner, the men will talk, drink tea and perhaps whisky, some will smoke opium. The women cook the pigs food and make clothes . Shortly after dark the family goes to bed.

About once a month for two or three days the men go hunting for bigger game in the jungle, perhaps bringing back squirrel, monkey, wild boar or deer.

The agricultural year.

1. Dry rice

After the New Year celebrations, the swiddens are prepared for planting. Trees are burned and undergrowth removed from January to the end of the dry season in the middle of April, when the seeds are planted in holes made by a dibber. Growth is rapid, and weeding is essential until harvesting in September, October or November.

2. Maize (corn)

Land preparation takes place in the dry season during February and March. Weeding is necessary until harvesting in September.

3. Opium Poppies

This crop must be planted at high altitude (above 1200 metres) on an east or north east slope. The fields will be near to the crest of a hill and shaded by trees. The poppy seeds are planted underneath corn which will have been growing in these fields. The corn shades the seedlings, aiding in their germination. After the corn crop has been taken the poppies grow rapidly throughout the dry season, getting moisture from dew and mist. They are harvested from late December to early March.

LAW AND ORDER

In the last twenty years, most of the hill tribe villages have become integrated into the Thai legal system. Every village, Thai or hill tribe, has a headman. Each headman is responsible to a local government officer in the nearest town, who will have overall responsibility for many villages. This pyramid of authority eventually reaches to the top levels of government.

The headman is therefore officially recognized and often appointed by local government, and is responsible to the authorities for the collection of taxes, registration of voters and other administrative duties. Frequently the Thai appointed headman will not be the same person as the traditionally appointed one, which may cause discord in the village. By Thai law, a headman must resign at the age of 60. This may cause problems for the village, since a new headman must be appointed when the allegiance of the villagers is often still to the older man.

Despite the problems that this co-existence between Thai and hill tribe produces, it is to the advantage of the hill tribes to co-operate with the government, since they will then be accepted as Thai citizens. They will then be issued with I.D. cards which give them security and other rights, such as to own vehicles and land. Minor crimes are dealt with by the villages themselves without outside intervention, which may be resented as unwarranted interference, but all major matters are dealt with by the Thai police and judicial system.

Traditionally, the position of headman was often one of great power. He could impose punishments ranging from fines to the death sentence. Depending on the tribe and the village, the headman could be the only arbiter of law and order, and could impose the law solely on his own judgment in some cases. He could benefit greatly from the imposition of fines, and if unpopular could hold onto power using force. Although today his legal power has been greatly reduced, he is still the main source of justice in local village matters, and his position is highly respected and can still lead to the acquisition of wealth. In order to effectively carry out his duties, in all but the smallest villages he will be assisted by one or more deputy headmen.

One problem caused by hill tribe tourism is the distribution of the money given, usually to the headman, by the trekking guides or tourists who stay overnight. The headman usually dictates in which houses visitors should stay, and receives a percentage of the money charged. Households who have few tourists to stay are liable to be jealous of more visited families. Fights and even the deaths of headmen or rich individuals have resulted from the strains produced by this new and unfamiliar source of income.

Below the headman in the legal hierarchy of the hill tribes there is usually some form of a 'council of elders', where the oldest male inhabitants, and in some instances the females too, meet to discuss current problems with the headman. This body may advise or instruct the headman in difficult cases, and effectively in most cases the headman is only able to function with their co-operation.

Village headmen meet, usually monthly, with the headmen of other villages, including Thai villages, in the nearest large town to take part in local government matters. This intercommunication with the dominant Thai culture is a valuable form of integration, one of the means by which the Thai government can achieve its aim of the Thai-isation and total integration of the hill tribes.

The village shaman does not have any direct control over legal matters. He does, though, have an important advisory function. Many crimes can be attributed, directly or indirectly, to the activities of evil spirits which may affect a persons actions. In these cases it is obviously important to consult with the shaman to discover which spirits are involved and what sacrifices to them may be necessary.

In some villages the headman will appoint a number of villagers whose function it is to see that the laws are obeyed and to oversee the punishment of offenders. Clearly, this is the equivalent of a village police force.

Punishments imposed vary from fines through banishment from the village to death. Banishment is a serious sentence, but commonly the banished persons will take some allies with them and form a new community or merge with another village.

The death penalty is very rarely if ever officially imposed by the headman today, except possibly in the most isolated communities. All crime serious enough for this will be dealt with by the Thai authorities. However it is not uncommon for a village to decide that a particularly dangerous or dishonest member of their community should have a fatal accident. Blood feuds have been reported in some areas, particularly in Lisu villages where the 'clan allegiance' system described later in this chapter can produce a number of warring groups.

In general, the incidence of crime within villages is low. Links between villagers are so close that it is very unlikely that any criminal will remain undetected, and the likelihood of upsetting the spirits and causing their wrath is a great deterrent.

AKHA

Every aspect of Akha life is strictly prescribed by a complex set of rules which can be translated as the 'Akha Way'. These rules combine religious and secular authority, and are deeply ingrained in every Akha. Rates of crime are therefore low.

The village headman is selected by a council of elders for his wisdom and experience, and is the repository of the 'Akha Way'. His functions, therefore, combine religion and justice.

Minor crimes are punished by the imposition of a fine, commonly given by the guilty party to the person wronged. In the past, women were beaten for the most minor offence.

For more serious crimes, banishment from the village may be imposed, or the ceremonial removal of a mans queue (topknot) of hair. This is a serious punishment, the public humiliation sometimes causing the death or insanity of the criminal.

Murder is regarded as a particularly terrible crime, and murder rates are very low. In the past, the murderer was beheaded after first having the hands removed.

LAHU

The Lahu headman has great, and in the past, absolute power over his village, although he is only maintained in office by the co-operation of a council of elders, who can also vote for his removal.

In times past, the Lahu headman appointed a number of 'po' who carried out the policing of the village and imposed sentences. Now, the local Thai police are likely to be used for this function.

All but the most serious offences are punished by a fine, always in units of 7 (traditionally silver rupees). Minor crimes include bad behaviour leading to divorce, allowing livestock to stray and damage another families property, and promulgating malicious gossip. Horse stealing is a serious offence, the guilty party having to pay a pig or cow in compensation. For adultery, the couple have their heads shaved and have to repeat 'do not do as we have done' until their hair grows back. Serious theft or witchcraft is punished by banishment from the village. The penalty for murder and some serious crimes was execution by beheading.

An important function of the headman is the ritual purification of the village to cleanse it of the crimes committed.

The Red Lahu have a number of 'tests of innocence' where an accusation is made and refuted. These are rare, since the guilty party will almost always 'own up' rather than face the test, which he believes will cause his death. Similarly, the accuser, if proved false, faces the same fate.

The commonest test involves the chewing of uncooked rice. The test will be ordered by the headman but officiated over by the shaman and attended by all the adult males of the village. A fence of wood or bamboo is erected from which carvings of the sun and moon are hung. A large pig is brought to the scene, to be paid for by the guilty party. The protagonists stand either side of the fence and fire a gun in the air. The loudest report is believed to come from the innocent parties gun. The final proof, though, is provided by the chewing of uncooked rice. After a few seconds of chewing,both parties spit the rice onto a leaf. The shaman decides which persons rice is more chewed, thus proving their innocence. The guilty party pays for the pig, half of which goes to the innocent party and half to the headman.He also pays a fine which is divided up between all the households in the village. It is believed that the guilty party will die within a few weeks.

Another test of innocence is the 'woodash' test. The shaman burns a

111

wooden stake and plunges it into a bowl of water. The suspect drinks the water and ash. If guilty, they will die within a short period of time.

LISU

The title of headman in a Lisu village is traditionally hereditary,but if the son is unsuitable an alternative will be appointed by a council of elders.

The Lisu headman has less power over his village than the headmen of other tribes. Most decisions are taken by the villagers themselves, who will resent and sometimes defy any interference. There are cases of the assassination of autocratic headmen who went a little too far in their attempts to control their villages.

Amongst the Lisu there is a very strong sense of what is right and wrong, and outside interference is regarded as unnecessary. A party who has commited a wrong will be 'shamed' into making the right form of penance or restitution. Instances where this form of justice is impossible are referred to an 'allegiance group', similar to a clan but not necessarily with kinship ties. There may be several of these groups in a village. Problems within each clan will be resolved by mutual agreement within the group. Problems between members of different clans are less easily solved, and if the headman cannot preserve the peace, feuding may break out between clans, which may lead to considerable bloodshed, and frequently results in one or more clans leaving to found a new village.

HMONG

Harmony and independence are the two maxims of the Hmong. They regard the judicial functions of a headman as largely unnecessary and will resent his interference in disputes unless it must be used as a last resort. For these reasons the powers of a Hmong headman are small, his function being largely advisory and ceremonial.

The position of headman is theoretically elected, but in practice heredity is more important. The Hmong tribe are divided into a number of clans (there are about 12 in Thailand, indicated by surname.) The headman will be chosen from the biggest clan in the village. The most powerful family within that clan will generally provide the headman. He is elected by consensus, and is usually experienced but not old - the Hmong favour a young, vigorous headman.

Disputes within clans are solved without the headmans interference unless his impartial judgement is specifically sought. The commonest source of disputes is marriage - non-payment of bride price, divorce, paternity, desertion etc. Since marriages are always between members of different clans (the wife joins the husbands clan), the role of the headman as an impartial arbiter is crucial. Even then, he will have to agree on his decision with the heads of all the households.

The headman only functions with the goodwill of the people of his village. He cannot impose himself on the autonomy of the clans and households or he will lose office. Although he has the power to decide disputes, he can only do this if his judgements are seen by the majority to be fair.

The headman's other role, usually but not always carried out by the same man, is to liase with the Thai authorities. Since the headmen of Thai villages have more power, this can cause problems. He may have to implement unpopular orders from the local authorities, such as the collection of taxes or recruiting villagers for road building. His inability to decide for the village without consultation makes his position between the two cultures sometimes very difficult. In practice, the Hmong ignore Thai authority as much as possible.

KAREN

The traditional Karen headman is appointed by the spirit world, so his position and functions are holy and venerated. In seeking a new headman the village shaman acts as a spirit medium and consults with the ancestors and local gods. Once chosen, it is believed that the headman's decisions come direct from the spirits.

In practise, succession is hereditary, but flexible. Usually the younger brother of the last headman is chosen. If there are no brothers, the headman's son takes over. In the unlikely event of no brothers or sons, another close relative will be selected.

The headman will be deposed if it is believed that he has lost contact with the spirits. A series of crop failures or the outbreak of disease in people or animals are taken as signs that the headman should be changed.

Politically, the headman resolves disputes, maintains order (often by threatening to call down avenging spirits on wrongdoers) and acts as a spokesman for the village in the outside world. The headman also decides when a village should be moved, and where it should be moved to. Karen villages are moved less frequently than those of other hill tribes, since they practice a semi settled form of swiddening with established fields which lie fallow for several years between cropping. The headman decides which households will farm which fields in any season.

A major cause of discord in Karen communities is that the Thai authorities will often appoint an official headman who is not the same as the traditional one. From the Thai point of view it is essential to have as headman someone who speaks Thai well, is literate, numerate and co-operative. These qualities may well be missing in the villagers choice, hence the problems.

MIEN (YAO)

Yao society stresses peaceful co-existence and non aggression. The Yao are generally a very friendly and polite people with a history of aristocracy and etiquette. Crime rates are very low, and the system of political organization is loose and ill defined.

The Yao headman is supposedly chosen for his intelligence, wisdom and experience, although the post has a strong tendency to be hereditary. His decision making powers are very limited, functioning more as the chairman of the more powerful council of elders.

The Yao have an interesting 'test of innocence'. The defendent is brought before the elders, and must retrieve a piece of silver from a bowl of boiling oil. If he can do this without burning his hands, he is declared innocent.

OTHER TRIBES

The peoples described in this section are not regarded as 'major hill tribes' for a variety of reasons. Some have become so integrated into Thai society that their cultural differences have all but disappeared. Others are isolated or their populations are very low. Two groups, Yunnanese and Shan, are not 'hill tribes' as such, but inhabit many upland villages.

The inhabitants of Northern Thailand are a mixture of many races which have integrated and inbred over many years to produce the people we think of as 'North Thai'. Many of these groups were, in the past, hill tribes themselves who became absorbed into the dominant culture. The six hill tribes described earlier in this book are distinct and culturally largely independant of the Thais, but other tribes have become so integrated that their individuality has largely disappeared. Ask a member of the Lawa what his race is and he is likely to say 'Thai', although aware of his different ancestry to other Thais. Other peoples of the hills, although not strictly hill tribes, are distinct groups. The Yunnanese from Southern China have many upland settlements. The Shans, whose villages are often quoted in trekking tours, are indistinguishable from Thais, although they may have migrated into Thailand from Shan state in Burma.

As the population of Thailand expands, lowland Thais are starting to farm the hills, and upland Thai villages are not uncommon in some areas.

There is little doubt that the gradual Thai-isation of all the hill tribes will continue and further blur the boundaries between different peoples. Intermarriage between hill tribe and Thai is no longer uncommon, and marriages between members of different hill tribes are starting to take place. Whilst it is sad that these forces will inexorably lead to the loss of much of these hill tribe cultures, it is an inevitable part of that cultural evolution which has been taking place since man appeared on earth. Whilst we, as visitors, might regret the gradual abandonment of traditional costumes and beliefs, there is no doubt that from the point of view of the hill tribes themselves they are given up voluntarily to be replaced with something better. Modern acrylic materials are much showier and easier to use than the old natural materials.The traditional Akha bodice is very hot to wear, so why not change to the much more practical sarong ? The Hmong house with dirt floor is difficult to clean and quickly becomes dirty, hot, and smoky. Is it fair to complain when Hmong people start to build far more comfortable Thai style houses ? Western medicine is seen by the hill tribes to be more effective than traditional Animist curing rituals, so it is not surprising to see the old ceremonies disappearing.

In the past, the hill tribes were fighting against hostile peoples and governments. Hence the fierce independence and remarkable costumes- a gesture of separateness to the dominant race. The Thais have welcomed and helped these people, so the reasons for their separateness have gone. Their gradual adoption of Thai culture can be seen as a sign of their increasing confidence and security.

LAWA

The Lawa are now confined to the plateau between and to the east of Mae Sariang and Mae Hong Son. They have a very long history of settlement in Thailand, stretching back perhaps 2000 years, although some claim to have come from Kampuchea 200 years ago. Others believe themselves to be the founders of the city of Chiang Mai, which they lost to the advancing Thais. Their own origins are uncertain. If not interbred with Thais they do not have mongoloid features, are taller than Thais and have more body hair - the males sometimes growing beards. It is probable that they originated from the south, and are possibly related to the Micronesians of the eastern Pacific. They have a legend that they were chased into their new homeland by a giant boulder which still sits in the river. When passing it, Lawa people do not speak in case it recognizes them and chases them again. Their language is related to that of the Wa of Burma.

Most Lawa are Buddhist, but with a strong Animist element added to it. They still make sacrifices of chickens, rice and buffalo to the spirits of their dead ancestors, and use the services of a shaman for this. Spirit cords worn around the wrist and ankle protect against evil and bad luck.

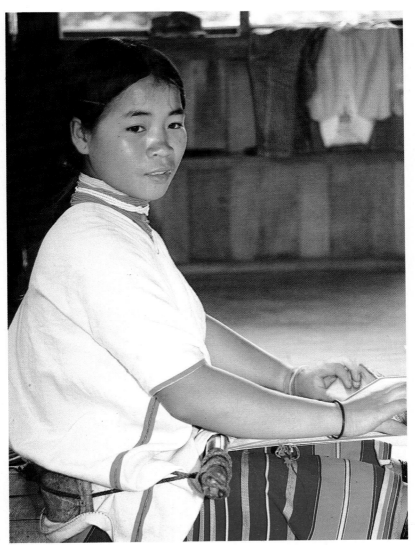

The Lawa only wear traditional costume in the most remote villages. Perhaps the original colonisers of north Thailand, they are now restricted to the mountains of the Mae Sariang area. Their claim to be the founders of Chiang Mai is backed up by some sound anthropological evidence.

The traditional costumes of the Lawa are beautiful. Unmarried girls wear white blouses, when married this is changed to fawn. The skirt is bright blue with horizontal bands of red, black and white. Many strings of bright orange beads are worn around the neck. Typically a large number of ankle rings are worn. Like the Pwo Karen, most adult women smoke a pipe.

Lawa villages are usually situated at an altitude of between 1000 and 1200 metres. Houses are of the traditional Thai style, and the structure of the village also follows the Thai pattern.

KHA-MU

The Kha-mu are found only in Northern Nan province. Their biggest settlement area is west of Rai, close to the Laos border. It is believed that in the past they migrated from Thailand to Laos and have recently moved back into Thailand. Their language and culture shows great similarities to that of the Lawa, and it is likely that the two populations were separated when the Thais moved into this area. Most Kha-mu have become absorbed into Thai culture through interbreeding and the adoption of Thai religious and social customs.

Their religion is a mixture of Buddhism which overlies their old Animist beliefs. They still believe in a multitude of spirits which they make sacrifices to, and many villages are entered though spirit gates. Some Kha-mu have recently become Christians.

Villages and houses are of Thai design, at an average altitude of 1000 metres. They are situated close to a stream or river.

They practice wet rice cultivation where possible, and the cultivation of tea. The men frequently work as labourers, and are likely to travel great distances to find work.

The traditional costume, rarely seen now, is of an embroidered skirt and sack blouse with heavy earrings and strings of beads.

H'TIN

The H'tin are restricted to a few areas close to the Laos border in Northern Nan province. They are a shy people, often not outwardly friendly to

A Phi tong Luang (Mlabri) hunter resting in the jungle. With no apparent hopes and little culture they appear to be the most abject of peoples - or have they reached that freedom from craving that Buddhists call the 'perfect' state of Nirvana?

outsiders, since they believe that foreigners bring bad spirits into the villages with them. They have gradually adopted Thai ways and customs, more through emulation than contact.

They are Animists, but have adopted Buddhist practices. A few have embraced Christianity. They make sacrifices to spirits and guard the entrance to their villages with spirit gates.

Villages are well designed in the Thai pattern, at an average altitude of 1000 metres. Houses are large and usually well built of wood or bamboo on stilts.

The womens costume is now rarely seen, but consists of woven skirts in bright colours, traditionally red, yellow and black.

They practice swidden rice agriculture and the cultivation of tea plantations. A few H'tin produce opium at the highest altitudes.

YUMBRI

Also known as the 'Mlabri' or 'Phi Tong Luang' (spirits of the yellow leaves), these people are the most fascinating and least understood in Thailand. Little is known of their customs or origins, and their numbers are very low - at present there are believed to be only 140, all living in remote mountain jungle in a few isolated areas of Nan province.

It is possible that the Yumbri are a race of people who have degenerated to their present level of existence. Their language is related to the Wa, Lawa and Kha-mu, so it is possible that their origins where with one of these tribes.

The Yumbri do not practice any agricultural techniques, but are hunter-gatherers, living off the produce of the forests which they inhabit. They are said to be efficient hunters, using long (4 metre) stabbing spears to bring down wild boar, deer, bear and monkeys. They also gather fruit, seeds, nuts and honey, and dig for roots which they exchange for tools and clothing in hill tribe (particularly Lahu) villages.

They appear to have no religious beliefs. The dead are quickly buried without ceremony and the tribe rapidly leaves the area of the death. They do not believe in any continuance of the spirit after death. The Thais and other hill tribes often think of the Yumbri as evil spirits, and

The H'tin used to believe that strangers brought evil spirits into the village. Although now mainly Buddhist or Christian, H'tin people are still reserved with strangers. This old lady is doing her best to ignore the camera.

121

in the past would shoot them. For this reason the Yumbri shun contact with other peoples.

They have no permanent settlements, staying in one place for at most 10 days. They build simple lean-to shelters of leaves over a ridge pole under which they sleep. When the leaves yellow, they move on.

They have no costume and may go totally naked in the jungle. When seen, they have usually been wearing a simple loin cloth. They are skilled at making rattan mats for barter, and make and play simple bamboo flutes. All their tools and utensils are made of wood or bamboo, although now they use metal which they receive from other hill tribes. They appear to be one of the most primitive tribes known in the world, with no art, language, religion or aspirations.

In recent years the Yumbri have started to work for local hill tribe farmers in exchange for food, clothes and tools, and very recently have learned the use of money.

Currently there is a plan to take a Yumbri family to Chiang Dao Resort as an 'exhibit'.

YUNNANESE

Called by the Thais 'Haw', these people are descendents of the inhabitants of Yunnan province in China. Yunnan has a long history of contact through trade with Northern Thailand, Laos and Burma, stretching back 2000 years or more.

Mule caravans from Yunnan brought such goods as velvet, brass, walnuts, porcelain, cooking utensils and lamps into Thailand, returning home with raw cotton, tea, opium and gemstones. Yunnanese settlements sprang up as the need for merchants and wholesalers in Thailand grew.

The mass migration of Yunnanese southwards, however, took place in two waves, following political upheavals in China. Many of the Yunnanese are Muslim, descendents of the followers of the Emporer Kublai Khan. In the 19th century the Muslims of Yunnan rebelled against the dominant Hans and set up an independant nation. When this rebellion was

A Yumbri couple. Dja and his 13 year old wife outside their simple bamboo and palm leaf house. They have been married two years and are content with their primitive style of life. Found only in the remotest areas of east Thailand, and numbering probably fewer than 140, this hill tribe shun society and its 'benefits'.

123

overthrown, many Muslims migrated to Thailand and Burma to avoid persecution, and set up farming or trading communities on marginal land the Thais did not use.

The second wave of migration took place in the 1950s, following the communist revolution in China. The followers of the ousted Kuomintang government fled to Taiwan, northern Thailand and Burma. They hoped to reinvade China, and built up an army for this purpose. To raise revenue, they traded opium and began the production of heroin, which they still do today, although with no hope of retaking China. There are many Kuomintang settlements in northern Thailand, the largest the fascinating town of Doi Mae Salong (Santikiree), north west of Chiang Rai.

Most Yunnanese in Thailand are now upland farmers, raising crops of corn, buckwheat, rice and cotton. They keep pigs and chickens. Villages are built in traditional southern Chinese style. Houses are low and built on the ground, often painted pink or green. There is a central guest room with bedrooms either side and a large kitchen at the back. Most villages have temples, which may be Buddhist, Taoist or mosques. The hillsides are dotted with graveyards in auspicious localities, the graves with plaster entrances leading to shallow underground vaults.

SHAN

Since they do not live in the hills and are not a tribe it may seem odd to include them in this book, but many treks will include a night in a Shan village in their itinerary.

The Shan peoples inhabit an area centred in Shan state, Burma, but extending into western North Thailand. In Shan state they have been rebelling against the government and demanding an autonomous Shan nation since Burma achieved independence. In Thailand they have been an intrinsic part of Thai culture for hundreds of years, and are indistinguishable from the Thais except in their appearance, which is less mongoloid and more delicate than the average Thai. This description, then, is as much about the culture of the Northern Thais as it is about a particular group called the 'Shan'.

Most Shan villages are close to the Burmese border. The towns of Mae

Sariang and Mae Hong Son contain a high proportion of Shan people. They speak a dialect of Thai called 'Thai - Yai' and show Burmese influences in their temple design and customs.

Typically, their villages are built in the lowlands or low foothills, usually near water and often in a bamboo grove. Houses are built of bamboo or wood on thick wooden poles of strong timber about 3 metres high. The nearest stream should flow east or north, the soil should be all of one colour and the spirits must approve. This is ensured by the rice grain test (this test is also used by many hill tribes). There will be a large living room containing a kitchen at the rear. There will be at least one large bedroom and sometimes a veranda . The area beneath the house functions as a workroom. The house and surrounding garden will usually be fenced off with bamboo.All villages rich enough will build a Buddhist temple.

Historically men who can afford to take more than one wife. This is now illegal under Thai law, but many men have 'minor wives' or concubines, although sadly, these women then have no legal status. A bride price must be paid by the groom, the amount depending on his wealth and the wealth of the girls family. Divorce is common, the assets of the couple are divided equally. Either side may keep any children, depending on circumstances. The wedding will normally take place in the brides parents house, officiated by a number of monks (usually nine since this is a lucky number). A monk will also choose the marriage date as being 'auspicious'.

At the birth of babies, the navel is tied with a thread and a silk scarf is twisted around its head. The mother is 'unclean' for seven days, then puts on clean clothes and returns to a normal life. All babies are unanimously declared ugly, to prevent spirits taking away their souls. After about 30 days the naming ceremony takes place, although illness or bad luck may cause the parents to change the name. At puberty, many boys will be tattoed to signal their emergence into manhood. Old people are highly respected.

The religion of the Shan is Buddhism, but most people still believe in a multitude of spirits. Death is followed by re-incarnation, to a higher or lower form of life, depending on how good the individual has been during their life. As good slowly triumphs over evil, it is believed that there is generally an upwards flow of reincarnations, culminating in the state of 'nirvana'.

After death the body is dressed in good clothes, traditionally with tears in them so that the spirit can escape. The body is watched for three days, at which time the spirit, which has been hovering between the human and spirit world, finally leaves. Chanting and the crashing of gongs continues until the body is buried. Mourners at the funeral wear bright colours. The coffin is carried on poles and covered with tiers of umbrellas. Monks precede the procession holding paper streamers attached to the coffin.

The traditional costume of the Shan is rarely seen except at ceremonial events. The women wear a long pale blue jacket with a standing black collar and cuffs of red edged with yellow. A black turban is worn on the head, with stripes of yellow, red, white and green. The edge of the turban is trimmed with gold.

The men wear baggy dark blue cotton trousers and matching blue shirts. Sometimes a cummerbund is worn.

TOURISTS AND THE HILL TRIBES

Tourism amongst the hill tribes of northern Thailand is a relatively recent phenomenon. The more accessible villages were reached over twenty years ago, but there are still villages in the remotest areas which have never seen a westerner. The organization and advertising of hill tribe tours is still largely controlled by Thais, there is as yet little interest from the big western travel agents, so tribal tourism is small scale, unsophisticated and inexpensive. Facilities on the tours and treks are basic, there is no attempt to coddle, so its appeal is largely to the young and slightly intrepid tourist. There are enough of these for the trips to make a reasonable profit for local tour agencies, but no way to produce the large profits needed to make hill tribe tourism attractive to the major western agents.

The typical hill tribe tourist, then, is fairly young, single, travelling cheaply through Asia, staying in cheap local hotels or guest houses, eating at outdoor food markets, trying to live within the local culture rather than observing it. He or she will be a student, teacher or professional person who has taken several weeks or months off to 'see the world'- the modern equivalent of the Victorian grand tour. They will be interested in 'experiencing' the culture they are seeing, although in moments of weakness they will buy a 'western' breakfast or seek out a Macdonalds burger, and delight in watching old movies on video. They will tend to be very environmentally aware and try very hard not to be patronising in their attitudes to the locals. They may prefer to be called 'travellers' rather than tourists. They will probably have experimented with illegal drugs, perhaps looking towards a hill tribe trip as an excuse to sample opium and marijuana cheaply and openly.

Most tourists arriving in Thailand are unaware of the existence of the hill tribes. Since Chiang Mai is the second city of Thailand, many tourists visit and only then decide on a hill tribe trek.

To appeal to the type of tourist described above, the tour agencies need to project an appealing, unique image upon the traveller. The hill tribes, of course, are not promoted by themselves, but by the Thai agents. The hill tribes are portrayed as living a life close to, and in tune with, nature. They are put forward almost as 'noble savages' living in a quaint and fascinating way, untouched by western civilisation. The sight of a plastic plate, transister radio or T shirt spoils this image for most tourists. If too many of these are seen, the village is 'spoilt' and the agencies are always looking for new, more remote and untouched communities to exploit. Nearer the cities, manicured hill tribe villages, whose populations depend almost entirely on tourism, are the alternative for the less adventurous, more comfort conscious tourist.

As communications, especially roads, improve in northern Thailand, more villages become accessible without the need for exhausting treks through the hills, so it is possible for the more sedate middle aged tourist to experience the hill tribes. Their limitations are likely to be time rather than money, so the comfort and speed of a coach trip to a hill tribe village is appealing, and profits to the tour agent correspondingly larger. These tours tend to be organized by the larger, more prestigious Thai travel companies, often acting as agents for western travel companies.

For the generally younger and fitter 'traveller' with plenty of time and not much money, the physical effort of the trek to remoter areas adds to the challenge and satisfaction. Some of these may organize treks themselves, with the considerable risk of robbery or death, not from the villagers, but the bandits who operate in some areas. Without a guide, they are unlikely to be aware of the etiquette and taboos of the tribes, causing animosity and a poor relationship between the tribes and westerners. Most of the younger trekkers pay for the standard jungle tour. Three or four days, staying in the villages of two or three of the hilltribes. Usually included will be an elephant trek for half a day and a days rafting down a river. For the majority of these tourists it is a worthwhile and deeply enjoyable experience. The authenticity of the villages is rarely questioned, nor the economic links between the tour guides and the villages.

Hill tribe tourism is not conducted for the benefit of the hill tribes. They have no say in its organization or regulation. They are simply an attraction, a useable resource, a source of profit, albeit meagre, for the tour companies. Interaction between the villagers and the tourists is not encouraged or desirable, as this may spoil their integrity and therefore their usefulness. You may feel, amongst the hill tribes people, that you are in a human zoo, but not be quite sure which side of the bars you are on at times.

The peoples of the hill tribes are generally hospitable towards strangers- it is an important part of their culture, as we have seen. Their first contacts with westerners, however, caused much fear and consternation.

With further contact, it became apparent that the tourists meant no harm, and a sequence of changes in attitudes took place. At first, tourists were treated with traditional, and lavish, hospitality-attempts at payment would be refused. Further contacts led to benevolent but passive indulgence. This may be followed by exploitive attempts to take advantage of the tourist, by begging or the hard selling of handicrafts. Finally, the most visited villages become dependant on tourism, devoting all their efforts to the manufacture of artefacts to sell to the tourist. This last stage has only happened in the most accessible villages which may have several hundred visitiors a day.

On the jungle tour, visitors stay overnight and are not separated from the tribesmen, who may be sleeping in the same house, usually the headmans, as would any other guest. The host family will probably cook for the tourists, but they will be segregated in a separate room. There will probably be little interaction between tourist and villager, apart from singing or dancing performed for the tourists by villagers, and sometimes vice versa. The main barrier is language. None of the villagers is likely to speak any European language-few speak Thai. The guide is the only source of information, and is likely to be selective in what he says, but will usually explain to the tourist the basics of the hilltribe life and beliefs.

The guide is of great importance to the hill tribe as well as to the tourist. He will prevent friction between villager and tourist by explaining the importance of correct behaviour and taboos. He will negotiate the terms on which the group stays with the village-where they stay, what food is to be cooked, what payments are to be paid and to whom. To the villagers, the guide is an important link with the outside world. He brings regional, national and foreign news, current development and fashions and often modern goods that the villagers will not have seen before. He frequently brings photographs of previous trips which many of the villagers are eager to see. In some villages the people are eager to have their photographs taken as they know they are likely to see themselves the next time the guide visits. If tourists become too common an event, however, the emphasis of the tourists becomes less an interesting diversion and easy source of cash for the villages, becoming instead a routine carried out solely for financial gain.

Villagers may come to see themselves as anachronistic curiosities, performing quaint tricks for the curious foreigners. Their belief in the value and depth of their own culture may be undermined, ultimately destroying it. This is not to anyones advantage, and tour agencies try to avoid the over exposure of all but the most blatantly exploited 'show villages'.

There are both potentially beneficial and harmful consequences of hill tribe tourism. There is no doubt that the small amount of cash which reaches the hill tribes through tours and the sale of handicrafts is a useful contribution to their income, and may reduce the debt problem with all its damaging effects.

Apart from the few villages subject to intensive tourism, there has not as yet been a great touristic impact on the culture of the hill tribes, although some problems have been created or aggravated.

The interest of many tourists in opium tends to aggravate the drug problem in the hills. In some tribes, opium addiction in adult males is over 30%. This is a major cause of ill health and loss of earnings, and contact with eager westerners gives many of the villagers a more positive image of the drug and tends to increase addiction. The cash derived from the sale of opium to tourists is frequently used to support the drug habit of the dependent villagers so aggravating the situation.

Tourists bring to the hilltribes direct contact with the western world and western values. The most obvious manifestation of this is the machine produced consumer products worn and used by the tourists. Villagers may see these as highly desirable, spending what little cash they have on them. Traditional clothing is being abandoned for western clothes, reducing the value of the traditional spinning and weaving crafts. There is a danger that the subsistence economy will decline as the hilltribes are pushed into the market economy in striving to obtain the cash to buy these consumer products.

There is also a danger that exposure to curious tourists may cause loss of personal dignity amongst highlanders. They may come to think of themselves as objects rather than subjects with a personality of their own, performing tricks for the tourist in return for a few coins. Begging is the worst example of this, but posing for photographs, mimicking foreign words and performing songs and dances without their normal ceremonial significance all tend to dilute the self worth of the hilltribes. If hill tribe tourism could be monitored and regulated to limit contact to an acceptable level, then it could be an acceptable and non damaging contribution to hill tribe economies. Without these controls, as hilltribe tourism expands, the societies which have survived for thousands of years, longer than any western culture, will gradually disappear.

OPIUM

Obtained from the sap of the opium poppy, Papaver somniferum, opium is an important cash crop to the Hmong, Mien, Lahu and Lisu. The drug has a fascination for many tourists. The common name for the region'The Golden Triangle'conjures up romantic visions of the exotic east-drug barons, smugglers and smoky opium dens of vice and addiction. In fact, opium is threatening the future of the hill tribes involved in its production. Amongst the Hmong, over 30% of the male population is addicted. The typical addict will smoke three or more times a day. They cannot work efficiently or at all, life expectancy is greatly reduced and families are pushed into malnutrition and misery. The production of opium has been illegal in Thailand since 1959, but despite all attempts by the govenment to persuade the hill tribes to change to other cash crops such as coffee, it is still produced in large amounts.

The advantages to the hill tribes of opium farming are that it has high

A young Akha opium smoker. The resinous ball of opium is moulded onto a hole in the pipe, a pin inserted and the opium smoke sucked into the lungs as it smoulders.

value for small volume, it can be stored without spoilage, the dealers come to the growers, and since it is only grown at high altitudes (above 1500 metres), there is no competition with lowland farmers.

Poppies and maize are usually grown in the same fields. Maize is planted in April and harvested in August. It provides feed for the animals and reduces the levels of soil pests. In September and October the poppy seeds are sown amongst the maize stalks that protect the young poppy plants. The crop must be weeded several times during its growth. It is harvested from mid December to the end of March. A few days after the petals have fallen, the outside of the pod is scored to the correct depth with a knife consisting of three sharp blades lashed together. The white sticky sap exudes from the pod and dries on its surface overnight. It oxidises to a brown gum which is scraped off with a broad bladed knife, formed into balls and wrapped in banana leaves or mulberry bark paper. Each pod can be tapped several times. The seeds from the best pods are kept for the next season.

Opium is the source of a wide variety of drugs given the general name of opiates. The most important include morphine, heroin and codeine. They are all powerful painkillers, but opium, heroin and morphine are highly addictive and tolerance quickly develops so larger and larger doses are needed. Depression of the higher centres of the brain causes feelings of euphoria in which fear, apprehension and inhibition are reduced, the ego is expanded and there is a general sense of well being. The user may experience a feeling of dreaming whilst still awake. Other less positive effects include nausea, sweating, drowsiness, mental and physical impairment, poor concentration, apathy, reduced hunger and lowered sex drive. In some individuals depression, anxiety and fear are produced. The opiates also suppress the activity of the muscles of the intestine, causing constipation or reducing the symptoms of diarrhoea. The respiratory centres of the brain are depressed, potentially causing respiratory failure and death.

The narcotic and sleep producing properties of opium have been known for thousands of years. The Sumerians in 5000 BC where the first to record its use. The Greeks used it extensively, Hippocrates noted its effects and the Roman physician Galen was enthusiastic about its use. The Arabs introduced it to Persia, China and India in the early middle ages. In Europe, Paracelsus discovered laudenum, tincture of opium. Later paregoric, camphor combined with laudenum, was used to control diarrhoea. For two hundred years opium was regarded as a universal panacea. It was the only effective painkiller and the dangers of addiction were not realised until the beginning of this century.

In the latter part of the 18th century, Britain discovered a lucrative trade in opium. It was grown in British India and exported to China in exchange for gold and silver. This was used to purchase tea and silks for import into Europe. The trade was controlled by the British East India company but they did not carry the drug themselves as its use was banned in China. They used instead 'country traders' licensed by the company to bring goods from India to China. These traders sold opium to smugglers along the coast and passed the proceeds to the East India company. Opium addiction became so high in the mid 19th century in China that their efforts to restrict its imports led to two opium wars with Britain. In 1860 China finally agreed to import the drug and charged tax on it. By 1917 voluntary restrictions on its production finally ended the trade.

In the 19th century its use in Europe and America was widespread. Patent medicines commonly relied on it for their effectiveness, and many people in positions of responsibility were unaware that they were addicted. In fiction, Sherlock Holmes used it extensively, and many writers and artists believed it aided their creative abilities. In this century vigorous attempts have been made by most governments to prevent its abuse. Heroin addiction has spread rapidly. Originally a problem of metropolitan slums, its use has spread to the middle classes. Rapid tolerance development and dependency, and severe withdrawal symptoms, lead addicts into a spiral which frequently ends in criminality and death through overdose.

There are many reasons why tourists in the hill tribes should not experiment with opium, quite apart from its criminality. Many people smoking opium for the first time have an adverse reaction with severe psychological effects. After smoking opium just a few times you may suffer withdrawal symptoms such as general restlessness and an inability to sleep. The interest shown by tourists in opium affirms its benefits to the hill tribes and gives them an extra market for the drug, thus encouraging the

A Blue Hmong 5 year old girl with the opium poppies which are a major cash crop for many hill tribe villages and the cause of much addiction and misery throughout the world.

production of a crop which can do nothing but harm to the hill tribes in the long term.

The opium trade in Thailand is largely controlled by two organizations or 'armies'. The Shan state army was formed to establish an independent country in Burma. Shan is the largest state in Burma, and has for nearly 30 years been fighting for its independence. The funds for its weapons and manpower are provided by the production of heroin from opium, and there are many heroin 'factories' on or close to the Thai - Burma border. Recently, they have extended their activities to inside Thailand, meeting opposition from the Kuomintang (KMT). They control most heroin production in Thailand, and have an interesting history. The KMT was the government of China until the communist revolution of Mao Tse Tung. At that time the KMT leaders fled to Formosa, establishing the independant state of Taiwan. Six hundred KMT members fled to Burma, with the intention of mounting a two pronged attack on China with their colleagues from Formosa. The KMT recruited an army of six thousand men for this attack, but the combined forces never became strong enough to challenge the government of China. The KMT recruited men from the hill tribes, and still does. Their funds come from the production of heroin. Each year traders visit the villages, buying up their opium at a low price. KMT 'caravans' then travel through the area, heavily armed, collecting the opium. Perhaps half of all opium produced in Thailand is bought by the Shan army and KMT. The opium is converted to heroin by a form of 'cooking' and the use of chemical catalysts. Six kilograms of opium provides 1 kilogram of heroin. The activities of the KMT have, in the past, been tolerated by the Thai government, since the KMT helped put down a communist rebellion within Thailand, and has provided a valuable service in patrolling the Burma border, preventing the infiltration of communist forces. This has also been seen as valuable by some western powers. In recent years the Thai army, helped by western funds, has become more efficient and Thailand does not need the help of the KMT so much. As heroin addiction has grown in the west, other governments have found it harder to turn a blind eye to KMT activities which may therefore be going through a period of decline. The present anti opium attitude of the King and the government is leading to more strenuous and efficient actions by the Thai army.

HILL TRIBES LANGUAGES

The languages of the hilltribes are as different from each other as the languages of European countries. Hmong and Karen are as similar as English and Russian. The only generalisations that can be made are that all hilltribe people speak softly and slowly, they have no general terms of greeting or leaving (no hello or goodbye) and lack words that we may regard as essential; for example most tribes have no word for food in general - since they eat rice at every meal, the word for rice means food. The English translation of the words and phrases in this section are as phonetic as possible. Little attempt to explain pronunciation is included, since this would be very difficult to master. Try out a few words after listening to the language as spoken in that tribe, be prepared for laughter and looks of amazement, and experiment with a few changes of intonation until you see the light dawn. Even if you dont get very far, its fun trying, and will be much appreciated and enjoyed by the hilltribes people.

The six languages can be divided into two or three groups.

Hmong and Mien speak Austro-Thai languages. They are very different, but have a Chinese sound and intonation. The other tribes speak a Sino-Tibetan group of languages, originating to the North and West of Thailand. Lisu, Lahu and Akha are classed as Tibeto-Burman languages, the Karen languages having slightly different roots.

Within each tribe there are quite distinct dialect differences. Skaw and Pwo Karen dialects are so dissimilar as to be regarded by many linguists as different languages.

KAREN (PWO)   KAREN (SKAW¹)

	KAREN (PWO)	KAREN (SKAW¹)
Hello (where are you going?)	Lessu le (as in let)	
Goodbye (I am going)	Leelon	
Yes	Meesur (sur as in certain)	Uhh
No	Meeber	Dumaba
Thank you	Nibonitar (Ni as in knee)	Tola Blu
How much	Chi dulleh	Delow
Good	Gwee	Gay
Very good	Gwee ter ter (ter as in terror)	Gay dorah

KAREN(PWO)   KAREN(SKAW)

Village	ring paa	zee
House	dank	du
Guest room	sow	depan
Food (rice)	obee	may
water	tea	tea
tea	char	normal
girl	amung	homung
boy	akwe	pockwa saho
bed	meenon	
baby	poesur	
beautiful	gweek	
What is your name?	Ami nit alair ?	me dee low?
1	Bon	De
2	Key	Ke
3	Saar	Sur
4	Lee	Lui
5	Yeah	Zer
6	Who	Chu
7	Noair	Noay
8	Kho	Chor
9	Quee	Quee
10	Lachee	Chee
20	Queechee	Queechee
100	Lapang	Dukuzar

LAHU

Hello (How are you?)	Sheyeh sa la (sa as in sarcasm, la as in alarm)
Goodbye (I am going)	nga gaye wee
Yes	Uhh
No	Mahe
Thank you	A bo u jar (bo as in boat, u as in blue)
How much	Kom a le (le as in leg)
Good	Dahdjar
Very good	Dahdehr

LAHU

Village	Kha
House	Yeah
Guest room	Hallah cho u la
Food (rice)	Djakar
cooked rice	Or
Water	Eka
Tea	Char
Boy	O ka ba
Girl	Yam eh ute
What is your name ?	Noh o meh at ma melley

1	Dee
2	Knee
3	Se (as in set)
4	Oo (as in not)
5	Nga
6	Koh (as in cock)
7	Ssuu
8	Hee
9	Caw
10	Teechee
20	Kneechee
100	Deeloy

LISU

Lisu people do not say hello or goodbye-there is no expression for greeting or leaving. If they want to leave they just go without saying anything, which can make us feel rather disconcerted.

Yes	Sue
No	Nusus (nu as in gnu)
Thank you	A kur bu mo (bu as in but, mo sa in moat)
How much	A mia
Good	How
Very good	Aker how
Village	Jazzer

LISU

House	Hee
Guest room	Etago
Food (rice)	Tza
Water	Igya
Tea	Chayeh
Cigarette	Yuko
Boy	Zuga
Girl	Yumuleh
What is your name	Nouz emir a lay bay
1	Ti
2	Ngi
3	Su
4	Lay
5	Knee ha
6	Cho
7	Shair
8	Heigh
9	Gu
10	Tssur
20	Nyissur
100	Tehaya

AKHA

Hello (where are you going)	Gala had yu dumgna
Goodbye	Oima (o as in oat)
Yes	Nngme (e as in met)
No	Mungu
Thank you	Galagumnya
How much	Am mian ngi
Good	Yomu
Very good	Yomu yu
Village	Nama pu
House	Yum
Guest room	Bollo po (o as in pop)
Food	Onyeu
Rice	Haw

AKHA

Water	Eacheu
Tea	Lobor
Boy	Alee
Girl	Abow
What is your name	Naw chumya you kontey
1	Dee
2	Nee
3	Sohm
4	Ur
5	Nga
6	Kho
7	See
8	Yeah
9	Whirr
10	Che
20	Niche
100	Teeyar

HMONG

The most difficult of the hill tribe languages to pronounce, all words end abruptly as if cut off, and most end in a rising intonation. From a distance, a conversation in Hmong sounds rather like a bad sneezing attack.

Hello (where are you going)	Ka yo mung two?
Goodbye (come back again)	Teha sang loo
Yes	Uhh
No	Yong
Thank you	Wud djow
How much	Bee tcho
Good	Yung
Very good	Yung dow dow (ow as in down)
Village	Yay yo
cigarette	Mouli
House	Djay
Guest room	Chewn nya

HMONG

Food	Tzow
Rice	Ma (as in mark)
Water	Gli
Tea	Chewa
Boy	Nua to
Girl	Nuang tsigh
What is your name ?	Bay who djam?
1	Ee
2	Oar
3	Pay
4	Blau
5	Tjur
6	Tjoa
7	Tchian
8	Yi
9	Tjiaw
10	Khao
20	Nen ngau
100	Ee pwa

MIEN (YAO)

Hello (where are you going)	Moi ming hai ?
Goodbye (I am going)	Yezzerno
Yes	Tseynya
No	Ummai
Thank you	Liang tsing
How much ?	Betear nyan
Good	Longhay
Rice	Mhay
Water	Wom (as in woman)
Tea	Tsar
Boy	Don
Girl	Shia
What is your name ?	May hew hoonyong ?

MIEN (YAO)

1	Yeeyet
2	Ee
3	P uwa
4	Pay
5	Dya
6	Tchu
7	Seea (a as in cat)
8	Het
9	Dua
10	Teaup
20	Neeteaup
100	Yupa

BIBLIOGRAPHY

Ethnographic Study Series (1970)	Minority Groups in Thailand *Cultural Information Advisory Service*
James W. Hamilton (1976)	Pwo Karen: At the Edge of Mountain and Plain *American Ethnographic Society*
W.R. Geddes (1976)	Migrants of the Mountains *Clarendon Press*
Labour, Hickey, Musgrove (1964)	Ethnic groups of mainland South East Asia *Human Relations Area Files Press New Haven*
Peter Kunstadter (ed.) (1978)	Farmers in the Forest *University of Hawaii*
Peter Kunstadter (ed.) (1967)	Southeast Asian Tribes, Minorities and Nations *Princeton University Press*
Lewis and Lewis (1984)	Peoples of the Golden Triangle *Thames and Hudson*
J. McKinnon/W. Bhruksasri (1986)	Highlanders of Thailand *Oxford University Press*
Tribal Research Institute (1989)	The Hilltribes of Thailand *Tribal Research Institute University of Chiang Mai, Thailand*
A.R. Walker (1981)	Farmers in the Hills *University of Malaysia*
O.G. Young (1961)	The Hilltribes of Northern Thailand *Government of Thailand and the United States of America Mission To Thailand*

INDEX